on track ...

YES

1968-1991

every album, every song

Stephen Lambe

SONICBOND

sonicbondpublishing.com

Sonicbond Publishing Limited
www.sonicbondpublishing.co.uk
Email: info@sonicbondpublishing.co.uk

First published in the United Kingdom 2026
First published in the United States 2026

British Library Cataloguing in Publication Data:
A catalogue record for this book is available from the British Library

ISBN 978-1-78952-652-3

Typeset in ITC Garamond Std & ITC Avant Garde Gothic
Printed and bound in England

Graphic design and typesetting: Full Moon Media

Follow us on social media:
Twitter: twitter.com/SonicbondP
Instagram: www.instagram.com/sonicbondpublishing_/
Facebook: www.facebook.com/SonicbondPublishing/

Linktree QR code:

on track ...

YES

1968-1991

every album, every song

Stephen Lambe

SONICBOND

sonicbondpublishing.com

For Chris Squire, Alan White and Peter Banks, wherever they are.

Acknowledgements

Special thanks also to Oliver Wakeman, Jon Anderson, Bill Bruford, Steve Howe, Billy Sherwood, Jon Davison, Rick Wakeman, Trevor Rabin, Trevor Horn and Geoff Downes for occasional moments of in-person insight, and to Jerry Ewing of *Prog* magazine for helping me meet some of my heroes.

Thanks to Bruce Strickland for sharing his ticket stubs and Yes programmes.

Thanks, as ever, to the Prog Widow – my gorgeous wife Gill.

Preface To The Third Edition

Yes formed in 1968. A few acts from that era are still with us – The Rolling Stones being a case in point, Dutch masters Focus being another, but I can think of no other group of musicians that are as phenomenally active as Yes.

When the first edition of this book was published at the end of 2018, Yes had just been inducted into the Rock and Roll Hall of Fame. Chris Squire had left the planet three years previously. It seemed that this might be a good point to close the door on the band and sum up a magnificent career. The short-lived Anderson, Rabin, Wakeman 'version' of Yes also called it a day that year.

But that wasn't the end at all.

First of all, the band Yes, led by Steve Howe – 79 years old at the time of writing – continued to both tour widely and – astonishingly – release new music, despite the untimely death of Alan White in 2022 and a pandemic that closed the entire world for more than a year. Secondly, Jon Anderson – in the Yes wilderness since 2008 – joined a band of Yes fanatics called The Band Geeks, and released an album in the spirit of his former band to universal acclaim.

Furthermore, in 2023, the Warner Group acquired all of the band's releases on Atlantic (up to *Big Generator*) and all associated compilations and live albums, while in 2024, all the post-2000 albums (from *Magnification* onwards) were acquired by Mercury Studios (a subsidiary of Universal). Technically, this left only the 1990s albums – *Union*, *Talk*, *The Keys To Ascension* and *Open Your Eyes* – without a major-label home, but with plans in the works nevertheless, with *Talk* re-released in 2024.

A second full edition of *Yes On Track* was published in 2023, bringing the story up to *Mirror To The Sky*, but it eventually sold out as well. This left me with a dilemma. Should I keep the book as a single volume and perhaps cut back some extraneous material to include the two releases in 2026, namely the reissue of *From A Page* and the new album from the current lineup, *Aurora*?

The problem was that I had never given the band's extensive, ever-expanding live catalogue enough attention, especially as archive releases from the 1970s are being released at quite a rate. In the end, the decision was made: the book would be split into two volumes. The first (this one) would deal with the 'classic' period up to and including the *Union* tour in 1991. The second would discuss the period from 1994 and the release of *Talk* right up to the present day.

So here it is. Part One – revised and expanded.

on track ...

YES

1968-1991

Contents

Introduction 11
Cast Of Characters (Up To 1991) 13
Yes Cover Art 19
Yes (1969) 22
Time And A Word (1970) 28
The Yes Album (1971) 33
Fragile (1971) 39
Close To The Edge (1972) 45
Yes Live In 1972 And 1973 51
Tales From Topographic Oceans (1973) 55
Relayer (1974) 61
The Solo Albums 65
Yes Live 1975 And 1976 68
Going For The One (1977) 70
Tormato (1978) 74
Yes Live In 1978 And 1979 79
The Paris Sessions And Related Tracks (1979) 80
Drama (1980) 84
Yesshows (1980) 89
90125 (1983) 91
90125 Live 102
Big Generator (1987) 106
Anderson, Bruford, Wakeman, Howe (1989) 110
Union (1990) 115
What Happened Next? 122
Other Live Albums And Compilations 124
Bibliography 126

Introduction

Was there ever such a complex band as Yes?

By that, of course, I mean structurally complex. I can think of few groups that have had so many lineup changes, yet so many members who have left the band and later rejoined; a band that has had so many different methodologies and motivations for creating music; a band that has been so divided by inter-band politics and squabbles over money. Yet Yes are a group of musicians that, at their best, have arguably made some of the most spectacular and uplifting music ever created. It makes for a colourful story. Only for a couple of barren years in the early 1980s was there no band called Yes at all, and while other periods have seen the band dormant, someone – somewhere – was holding the torch. Musicians were planning, talking, or writing. And fans were waiting.

Author's Note

Somebody somewhere will write a book about every live version and every other variation of every Yes track. This is not that book and I have only referred to versions when I believe they add something to our understanding of the album in question. If you've bought a previous version of this book, however, you will note that I have now given wider consideration to the live albums released during this era. That said, I've still only included band-sanctioned releases, even if something of a grey area has grown up between 'official' releases and bootlegs.

Many of the Rhino remasters have studio run-throughs of some pieces, particularly the epics. I have not mentioned them here. In addition, you will find that this book is a bootleg-free zone. Dozens of bootlegs of the band – good and bad – have been released over the years, and, aside from the moral considerations, there is simply too much material to examine. The only exception to this is the BBC Recording of the Wembley Arena concerts in 1978. This has been mined for a few 'official' live tracks over the years, and I hope that we will see an 'official' release of the full set sometime in the future.

As mentioned, Yes (collectively) no longer own the recordings from most of this era. The group had already gone through a period of remastering and reissuing the albums via its Rhino label, but in recent years expanded reissues have begun to emerge, many of which will test the pockets of even the most hardened Yes completist. I'll touch on this to a certain extent, but buyer beware and bear in mind that no members of the band receive royalties from these new editions, even if they are consulted up to a point, as Steve Howe was with the reissue of *Tales From Topographic Oceans*, released in 2025.

While I haven't revised every single word in this book, each word has certainly been *assessed* for amendment. If you have my book about *90125*, you might find some of the song analyses familiar. I have lifted them lock, stock and barrel from that book, completely replacing the old analysis in this book. The exception is 'Owner Of A Lonely Heart', which is a shorter hybrid of both versions.

Nobody's perfect, least of all me, and if I have missed anything out that I really shouldn't have, then do contact me via the publishers so I can correct it for future editions. An email address can be found at the end of this book.

Above: A blue plaque denoting Yes' rehearsal space in London in 1968, prior to installation. (*David Watkinson Collection*)

Cast Of Characters (Up To 1991)

I cannot think of another major rock band that has had so many lineup changes. Even though King Crimson have reinvented themselves many times over the years, their lineups always revolve around one man, Robert Fripp. In the case of Yes, these changes have generally been more gradual, built around a group of musicians rather than just one. Until his death in June 2015, only Chris Squire had been in every incarnation of the 'official' band. Overall, 12 musicians were 'official' members of Yes during the timescale discussed in this book, so what follows are brief thumbnail sketches of them all.

Only 'full' members of the band have been included. Even this is moot, since in later years some members were probably on contracts rather than considered 'permanent'. My definition, therefore, is any musician who played live and was also involved in creating new music in the studio. Tony Levin has a good claim to full membership due to his participation in *Union*, but has not been included. I have also left out Eddie Jobson, who joined briefly in 1983 when Kaye left for a few months but decided not to stay. I have considered the band dissolved between 1980 and 1983, and despite my inclusion of the album in this book, participation in ABWH is not considered to be membership of Yes.

Jon Anderson (born 1944)

Vocals, harp, guitar, percussion. 1968-1980, 1983-1988, 1991-2008, 2017-2018 (ARW)

Born in Accrington, Lancashire, Anderson is felt by many fans to be the 'soul' of Yes, not only for his lyrics but also for his overall orchestration of the fortunes and music of the band, particularly in the early days. His relatively meagre skills as a musician set him apart from the virtuosity of the rest of the group, but his musical vision – as well as his unusual worldview – makes him one of the most singular musicians of his generation. And then, of course, there is 'that' voice – his unusual alto. He has rarely had problems with his voice, and singing the right note (i.e., pitching) has not been an issue since decent onstage monitoring became a 'thing' in the early 1970s. If you consider all those live recordings, he doesn't always sound like his voice is in great shape – perhaps too many dates into a long tour – but does he sing the wrong note? Hardly ever.

Outside of Yes, Anderson has had a varied solo career, and not always a successful one. He supposedly has as many unfinished projects as he has finished. He enjoyed a short but interesting career as a vocalist for hire in the 1980s, and his most prolific time as a solo artist was the early to mid-1990s. However, it was his career with Greek keyboard player Vangelis – himself one of the great sonic stylists of the 1970s and 1980s – that gave him the greatest success outside Yes. The duo released four studio albums and had two massive hit singles in the UK with 'I Hear You Now' and 'I'll

Find My Way Home'.

As for Yes, Anderson is a quirky character and supposedly not always easy to work with, and his relationships with Squire and Howe, in particular, were caught up not just in (allegedly) financial squabbles but also in personality issues that blighted the band from the late 1970s onwards. Yet, perhaps equal with Chris Squire, Anderson remains the most beloved of the Yes family, and it's not hard to understand why.

Chris Squire (born 1948, died 2015)
Bass, vocals, piano. 1968 -1980, 1983-2015
Alongside Anderson, Squire is widely regarded as the keeper of the Yes flame, and his death in June 2015 was met with understandable grief by many thousands worldwide. His nickname 'Fish' (not to be confused with the erstwhile Marillion vocalist) came, amongst other things, from his habit of taking enormously long baths. He was also constantly, and famously, late for everything. A chorister in his youth in London, Squire was tall, elegant and good-looking, with big hands that earmarked him for life as a bassist. However, he came at his chosen instrument from a supremely melodic angle, almost as a lead instrument. For me, his playing is a hybrid of the traditional bassist role – providing the 'bottom' – and a lead instrumentalist, offering the band unusual options when seeking that extra texture in an arrangement.

He usually played with a pick, and his main instrument in the early years, the Rickenbacker bass, with its famously accentuated 'high end', meant that he cut through the mix better than most bassists. In a nutshell, he is one of the most 'heard' bassists in history, with a technique that is completely different from that of the jazz-oriented players so popular in the 1970s.

His strong backing vocals, which complemented Anderson's so well, were also a crucial part of the band's character, particularly in a live setting.

Unlike Anderson, most of Squire's work was within Yes. He released a superb solo album, *Fish Out Of Water*, in 1975, and his collaboration with Billy Sherwood, Conspiracy, produced a couple of decent rock albums, too. But Squire will always be associated with Yes above anything – and almost anybody – else.

Peter Banks (born 1947, died 2013)
Guitar, vocals. 1968-1970
Banks was the first musician to leave Yes – ousted by Anderson and Squire – and it is clear that the anger and disappointment this produced never left him throughout what was a stop-start musical career. A talented and versatile player in his own right, he went on to form the groups Flash and Empire. Both bands showed promise but never fulfilled their potential, and his solo album *Two Sides Of Peter Banks,* which included a guest appearance by Jan Akkerman of Focus, also failed to live up to expectations. The debut album

by Flash – released in 1972 – is a rather spooky 'alternative Yes'. It features a more primitive progressive rock, looser and a little bluesier, considering that by then Yes were recording the groundbreaking *Close To The Edge*.

Banks had a career revival in the 1990s and 2000s as a solo artist and also in the improvisatory trio Harmony In Diversity, but these projects never rose above cult status. He was involved in early discussions to take part in revivals of both The Syn (with whom he had played with Squire prior to Yes) and Flash, but was ultimately excluded from both projects. His 2001 memoir, *Beyond And Before,* is an excellent read. Many of his recordings have been reassessed in recent years, and several have reappeared via the excellent Esoteric label. They are worth checking out.

Bill Bruford (born 1949)

Drums, percussion. 1968-1972, 1991-1992

It's hard not to admire this most enigmatic of percussionists. Born in Kent to a relatively well-off, middle-class family, Bruford has had a hugely varied and creative career, contrasting extreme pragmatism in his financial and organisational affairs with a desire to pursue art rather than untold riches. He developed his studied and very musical style of drumming while in Yes, then mystified the band by leaving just as the group were about to 'make it big' to join King Crimson. He also pioneered the use of electronic drums in the 1980s via a long-standing relationship with manufacturer Simmons, a texture he brought to Anderson, Bruford, Wakeman, Howe and his brief tenure back in Yes thereafter. However, for me, it is his solo band – Bruford – that was his most successful, musically, mixing jazz with rock in a very British-sounding fusion.

Later years were spent teaching and mainly playing the music that is his first love – jazz – via his band Earthworks, but there were many other, relatively low-key projects until his retirement in 2009. He has since refused to return to exhibit his perceived decline in musical powers in front of thousands of people each night for large sums of money. Unlike other members of Yes, Bruford has always had an unusually balanced view of his life, and a return to playing seemed very unlikely; when he did finally return, in the 2020s, it was to perform in a low-key jazz group, The Pete Roth Trio.

Tony Kaye (born 1946)

Keyboards. 1968-1970, 1983-1995

Handsome, enigmatic and private, Tony Kaye is probably the most underrated musician in the Yes family. The first two Yes albums show him to be a dexterous and inventive player, particularly on his favoured instrument, the organ. However, he seemed musically intimidated by the arrival of Steve Howe in 1970 and lost his place, as much for his unwillingness to embrace the new orchestral direction of that band as for any perceived lack of technique. Yet he has spent more time in Yes than Rick Wakeman, even if, during the *90125/Big Generator* era, he was little more than a live keyboardist, with Trevor Rabin playing many of the keyboards on those albums.

When outside Yes, he formed the band Badger, played live with David Bowie and did many sessions, going 'off radar' for years at a time. He also formed a strong friendship with Billy Sherwood, playing with him in the band Circa and touring as a duo. When the band received their Rock and Roll Hall of Fame award in 2017, he was the only living member of the band not to attend. He was involved in the 50th-anniversary celebrations and released his first solo album, *The End Of Innocence*, in 2021.

Steve Howe (born 1947)

Guitars, vocals. 1970-1980, 1991-1992, 1996-

There is little doubt that Howe is one of the most inventive and distinctive guitarists of his generation, with a style almost perfect for Yes. With his trademark hollow-body Gibson and his myriad of influences, including jazz guitarists Wes Montgomery and Les Paul, no guitarist sounds like Howe. He has kept himself fit over the years, too, and seems to be playing as well as ever, technically, but without the fire of the early 1970s. Howe's solo career has been interesting and pretty high on quality, whether playing full-on rock or acoustic pieces, and he has not been afraid to tour small venues on his own. He is an intense character who guards his hands and, as a result, can come off as reserved. He also retains his almost childlike love of music, as his large guitar collection demonstrates. His autobiography *All My Yesterdays* was published in 2021 and demonstrated his precision and love of the guitar far more than his desire to dish the dirt on his bandmates.

Beyond Yes, he was a founder member of two bands that attempted a more commercial rock style. Firstly, Asia – the hugely successful supergroup with John Wetton, Carl Palmer and Geoff Downes – and then GTR. This latter project was an attempt to link two guitar-playing Steves – Howe and Hackett – into a viable group, but with less success than Asia. Anderson, Bruford, Wakeman, Howe probably came at the right time for him, as did the invitation to rejoin Yes in 1996. Unusually, he has also embraced the 'tribute band' culture, playing live with the UK-based Yes tribute Fragile with some success in the mid-2000s.

Rick Wakeman (born 1949)

Keyboards. 1971-1974, 1976-1980, 1991-1992, 1996-1997, 2003-2004, 2017-2018 (ARW)

Wakeman's career is impossible to summarise in a single paragraph. By the time he joined Yes in 1971, he had already been a member of the Strawbs, played on countless recording sessions, including 'Space Oddity' and much of *Hunky Dory* by David Bowie. Between periods, in Yes, he became a huge solo star via a string of albums on the A&M label, such as *The Six Wives Of Henry VIII* and *Journey To The Centre Of The Earth*, a number one hit album in the UK. Life wasn't always so kind. He struggled with alcoholism and has married four times. He had his first heart attack in 1974. He has had various businesses over the years and has provided financial backing for the short-lived Mellotron update, the Birotron, but has otherwise had a close association with the Moog organisation and the Japanese company Korg.

A parallel career as a comedian and raconteur led to many solo tours, during which he could play music and tell colourful tales from his long life on the road. His performance of 'Life On Mars' following the death of David Bowie touched millions in the UK and led to an unintended upswing in his popularity as a pianist. In his 70s, his prodigious technique has never escaped him, and he remains as consistent and flamboyant a performer as ever. He has toured with his band The English Rock Ensemble, playing solo and Yes music in recent years, and has stopped playing one-man shows, preferring to tour with family members and friends, including another Yes alumnus, his son Oliver.

Alan White (1949-2022)

Drums, percussion, piano, vocals 1972-1980, 1983-2022. Died 2022.

Although only 23 when he joined Yes, White, originally from the North East of England, had already played with John Lennon's Plastic Ono Band, Alan Price and Balls with Denny Laine. Like Squire, most of his energy since was devoted to Yes, although he released two solo albums, one of which became a short-lived band, White. He also played with various bands in the Seattle area, where he lived until he passed away in 2022, and was also in Circa with Billy Sherwood. Around 1981, White joined Squire in the short-lived XYZ with Jimmy Page of Led Zeppelin before forming Cinema with Trevor Rabin, who later became, once again, Yes. His power and energy in the 1970s were astonishing, as live recordings and videos demonstrate. Health problems in recent years diminished his powers as a drummer, although he did play on *The Quest* and *Mirror To The Sky*.

Patrick Moraz (born 1948)

Keyboards. 1974-1976

Swiss keyboard wizard Moraz was the perfect choice to replace Rick Wakeman. He had previously played in the Swiss-based band Mainhorse and then in Refugee, effectively Nice, with Moraz replacing Keith Emerson. He fitted the bill with Yes perfectly, as his interest in jazz aligned with the band's direction as they composed material for *Relayer*. After Yes, he had a prodigious solo career, mixing musical styles including rock, jazz, electronica and South American music. He also had a piano-and-drum duo with Bill Bruford in the 1980s. Although he left Yes under strange circumstances, he continues a broad association with the band, appearing onstage during the 2018 50th anniversary celebrations and also appearing at *Cruise To The Edge*, the progressive rock pleasure cruise.

Trevor Horn (born 1949)

Vocals, bass. 1980-1981

Trevor's time as a member of Yes was only part of an association that led to him producing the *90125* album and working on the initial sessions for *Big Generator*. Originally the musical director for singer Tina Charles and then bassist and vocalist of The Buggles with Geoff Downes, Horn went on to produce countless top pop acts, including ABC, Frankie Goes To Hollywood, Art Of Noise and Dollar, and formed label ZTT with journalist Paul Morley. He is one of two members of the Yes family to have been honoured by the British establishment (the other being Rick Wakeman), having been given a CBE for services to the music industry.

Geoff Downes (born 1952)

Keyboards, vocals. 1980-1981, 2011-

Initially associated with Horn in The Buggles, the two went their separate ways after the *Drama* tour. Downes formed Asia with Steve Howe, John Wetton and Carl Palmer, catapulting them all to further success in the 1980s. Downes was the one constant member of Asia throughout the 1980s and 1990s, but he also worked as a producer for The Thompson Twins and GTR. He has also produced the occasional low-key solo album and formed an Asia side project called Icon with his long-term writing partner, John Wetton, in the 2000s. More recently, he formed a project with singer Chris Braide called the Downes Braide Association.

The original lineup of Asia reunited in 2006, and Downes also re-joined Yes in 2011. Remaining keyboard player in Yes is not an easy task, and Downes has proved surprisingly adept at playing in the styles of his predecessors, for which he should receive great credit.

Trevor Rabin (born 1954)

Guitar, keyboards, vocals. 1983-1995, 2017-2018 (ARW)

Rabin was a teen idol – and a guitar prodigy – in his native South Africa, best known for his band Rabbitt. Moving to London at the end of the 1970s, Rabin released three solo albums in the heavy rock/AOR vein, tapping into the spirit of the new wave of British heavy metal, also producing albums by Wild Horses and Manfred Mann's Earth Band during this time. A move to Los Angeles saw various opportunities come and go (including the chance to be in Asia), but he eventually found a path to Squire and White, and the rest (as they say) is history.

After an excellent solo album in 1988 called *Can't Look Away*, Rabin found himself involved in film scores and recording. In 2013, he released a very varied album of instrumentals, *Jacaranda*, and, of course, returned to Yes music via the Anderson, Rabin, Wakeman version in 2016. Another excellent solo album, *Rio*, was released in 2023.

Yes Cover Art

Roger Dean

The name Roger Dean is synonymous with Yes, and in the same way that the band's music has been much imitated, so has Dean's unique cover art and typography. With his remarkable curved Yes logo, with the 'tail' of the Y winding like a snake through the E and becoming the S from the bottom, he created one of the most iconic pieces of graphic art in rock music history.

Most bands change their typography over time, as indeed Yes did, but few have returned to one design, indeed one artist, as often as Yes have done over the 50-plus years since *Close To The Edge* was released. A myriad of other bands have used his art as a template for their own work. His designs have inspired books and movies, too, as those who have seen the huge Hollywood hit *Avatar* will testify.

The amiable and gentlemanly Dean designed the covers for an astonishing number of Yes albums, though not all of these albums are the best Yes recordings, nor are all of these covers his best work. Overall, his style can be considered 'fantasy art', but with many variations. Most recently, his work has moved towards fantastical landscapes with a greater realist edge. His paintings often play with perspective, so as the viewer looks closely, we realise that what he is depicting isn't physically possible, or at least topographically unlikely. While Yes have never been a 'cool' band, Dean's imagery has flirted with fashion from time to time. Sarah Jessica Parker even wore a *Tales From Topographic Oceans* t-shirt on an episode of *Sex In The City* in the early 2000s, while Lady Gaga can be seen wearing a Yes t-shirt in the 2018 version of *A Star Is Born*. As well as the iconic Yes logo, Dean's personal hallmark is the spacecraft depicted for *Fragile* – it appears whenever his name does on everything he designs.

It is four studio – and one live – albums for which Dean is most celebrated. Dean first worked with Yes after he sent a portfolio to Phil Carson at Atlantic Records, who employed him to design the cover of *Fragile*. Taking the album title as his inspiration, Dean envisaged a tiny blue-green world in a dark blue void, with a strange spaceship flying away from it. On the cover, the world is intact; on the back, the world is beginning to break up. The vinyl version also includes a booklet with Dean's paintings on its cover. Many of Dean's favourite features are apparent immediately – his love of exotic trees in unusual situations and paths that curve in and out of the picture are a particular feature.

Close To The Edge was even bolder, if deceptively simple. The first Yes album to include the famous logo, the cover is a single burst of green, shifting from dark to light from top to bottom. The gatefold, however, features an astonishing landscape – waterfalls cascading from a lake on all sides of a mountaintop. Where is the water coming from? A path snakes onto the lake from other mountaintops. Wherever you go in this world, you are ... Close To The Edge ...

Yessongs showed the eventual path of the fragments of the planet introduced in *Fragile*. For me, the brown front cover with its green tendrils of vegetation is his least successful. It is rather an odd mess, but the internal paintings are stunning, showing the segments travelling through space, landing in an alien sea and then in place in a misty landscape. Finally, we see the return of the spacecraft from the cover of *Fragile*.

If ever there was an album whose cover summed up and complemented its tone, it has to be the sumptuous gatefold painting that sits across the front and back of *Tales From Topographic Oceans*. The moon rises over an ancient pyramid. In the foreground, we see ancient stone piles, and yes, those are fish swimming through the atmosphere on the back cover. Deceptively simple yet awash with hints at mythology and evolution, it's a stunning piece of work.

Relayer is, too, a huge contrast, reflecting the war-like nature of the music. Two figures on horses ride into a huge cavern, while on the back, a snake curls menacingly. Does the snake represent evil? Aside from this detail, this is a Tolkien-esque image, yet its monochrome tones with just hints of colour in the snake are remarkable. This sort of cover is what vinyl was for, giving the listener an immersive experience by combining the music with the cover artwork in their imagination.

The late 1970s Yes albums controversially had covers that were designed by Hipgnosis, the agency that had made iconic album covers for Pink Floyd, but Dean made a brief comeback with a superb cover for the second live album *Yesshows* in 1979 and a painting for the 1981 compilation *Classic Yes* – an odd cover, this one, with an almost photo-negative feel – returning properly to Yes studio albums for the *Drama* album in 1980.

This painting is not my favourite, but it does have a sort of appropriate, almost abstract charm. His remarkable painting for *Anderson, Bruford, Wakeman, Howe* (1989) mixes the ancient with sci-fi using an almost photo-realist quality. This marks a period when Dean's paintings become decoration rather than an integral part of the album experience, with his name attached to a Yes-related project seeming more important than the paintings themselves. That said, his two paintings for *Union* are very impressive in his fantastical landscape style. Managed, like Yes, by QEDG, Dean remains closely linked to Yes to this day.

Other Cover Art

There was, of course, life before and between Roger Dean covers, and whenever the band felt the need to 're-invent' itself, Dean was ditched in favour of a new broom. *Yes* and *Time And A Word* were both given different covers for their UK and US releases. The first album has a simple 'speech bubble' design for the UK release, and a band picture for the US, while the same pattern was repeated with *Time And A Word* – an odd and rather unsatisfyingly abstract design in the UK and a simple band picture (featuring Steve Howe, who is not on the album) in the US. *The Yes Album* is distinctive, with its rather clichéd film-strip design and a low-light picture of the band and that disembodied mannequin head, which hung around as a band symbol for some time, even appearing on the *90125 Live* video. You also get Tony Kaye's ankle in a plaster cast.

Roger Dean, however, arrived at the right time, just as the band were starting to make commercial headway, but the changes were well and truly rung in 1977 when, after almost three years without a new Yes album, the decision was made to use the Hipgnosis agency for *Going For The One*. This is a striking cover, almost as iconic as the Dean paintings, but it has dated rather badly. A naked man (seen from behind) stares up at skyscrapers against a blue sky, while various lines criss-cross the picture. As an image, it 'parallels' the aspirational nature of the title track while also suggesting the track which closes side one. It is daring and distinctive, and the same can also be said of the follow-up cover for *Tormato*, although in a less impressive way. The title is a terrible pun, a play on Howe's chosen title YesTor (after the hill on Dartmoor, in Devon, UK), and the tomato that was thrown at the intended album photograph out of desperation, after it was rejected by almost everyone.

Incidentally, the tomato was either thrown by a Hipgnosis employee, or by Rick Wakeman, depending on which account you believe.

The sudden re-emergence of Yes in 1983 understandably brought about a complete re-invention of how the band was to be sold to the world, and the cover of *90125* is steeped in the quasi-modernist minimalism rife in 1980s design, with the cover shapes generated by computer. Unlike the music, thankfully. It's grey with some geometric colour patterns in the middle – and no Dean logo. The same approach was used for *Big Generator,* with its oblique reference to the *90125* cover, clearly intended as a new Yes logo of sorts. It didn't take, and Dean was back for *Union*.

Yes (1969)

Personnel:
Jon Anderson: vocals and incidental percussion
Chris Squire: bass, vocals
Peter Banks: guitar, vocals
Bill Bruford: drums, vibes
Tony Kaye: organ, piano
Produced at Advision and Trident Studios, London, between March and April 1969 by Paul Clay and Yes
Release date: July 1969
Highest chart places: none
Running time: 41:30

How did Yes come to be?

Many bands' initial incarnations are messy, and Yes' was no exception. Peter Banks and Chris Squire had played in The Syn between 1965 and 1967 with some minor success in London, but when that band folded, Squire was invited to join Mabel Greer's Toyshop, a psychedelic group fronted by guitarist and vocalist Clive Bayley and including drummer Robert Haggar. Squire brought in Banks, who initially stayed for only a few weeks. Squire had better connections, not least at The Marquee Club in Soho, so the band's profile began to rise.

Meanwhile, Jon Anderson, having returned to the UK after some adventures in Germany with his band, The Warriors, for three years, was looking for a band following a few abortive attempts, one of which was a couple of singles as a solo artist, Hans Anderson.

Squire and Anderson met at the Le Chasse club in London in spring 1968, where Anderson was in limbo. He invited Anderson to join the band. It's not difficult to imagine the ructions that must have caused, and within a few weeks Haggar had moved on and, finally, so had Clive Bayley. Haggar was replaced by the young and hugely talented (but not without experience) Bill Bruford, and with Banks now back in the band, the last piece in the puzzle was to bring in a keyboard player – Tony Kaye. The band changed its name to Yes. As with many things in the Yes story, the name of the person who chose the name of the band is disputed, but the most vociferous claimant was always Peter Banks, so who are we to argue?

The band started rehearsing in the basement of The Lucky Horseshoe Café in Shaftsbury Avenue. A blue plaque initiated by Yes author and collector David Watkinson can be seen at that location. They got their first big break when they stood in for The Sly and The Family Stone at a gig in the middle of September. This led to the gentlemanly Roy Flynn, who passed away in the early summer of 2026, offering to manage them.

It was not completely plain sailing, however. Under some pressure to go back to University, Bruford left, to be replaced by Tony O'Reilly and, for a while, by Ian Wallace, who had been in The Warriors with Anderson. It wasn't until Bruford saw the band with O'Reilly, who he thought was poor, that he agreed to rejoin.

Yes was recorded just four months after a pivotal gig at the Royal Albert Hall supporting Cream in their farewell concert. The band were still developing as a live act, although intensive rehearsals had gone a long way towards honing their skills, and they were developing a justified reputation as an exciting concert band, mixing reinvented, expanded cover versions with their own material. As a result, this first effort largely recreates the arrangements of many of the songs from that live set. They were allocated solid Atlantic house producer Paul Clay, though he seems to have been a new hire, and his credits before and after are fairly light. In typically ambitious fashion, Jon Anderson had wanted Paul McCartney. The final result is not at all bad. Six somewhat variable original tracks combine with two cover versions, although several other songs were also recorded and appear on the 2003 Rhino re-master.

Musically, the record is an interesting mixture of styles – from the unashamedly psychedelic calling cards of the two opening tracks and the Beatles cover (on side two) to the somewhat cloying 'Yesterday And Today' and 'Sweetness'. 'Looking Around' was clearly intended as the 'big pop single', while the two most interesting tracks are the proto-progressive rock pieces 'Harold Land' and 'Survival'. Indeed, it is not hard to work out why the band were so well thought of as a live act. Jon Anderson's voice was unique even then, and Chris Squire was already showing that swashbuckling bass style for which he became so famous. Bill Bruford comes across as an aspiring jazzman, very skilled yet not quite in possession of the precise style that would make him so famous in the 1970s. As for the other musicians, Tony Kaye remains, for me, the unsung hero of both this and its follow-up *Time And A Word*. His organ playing is powerful, melodic and dexterous, and his reputation as a 'journeyman' rests largely on his relatively safe performance on *The Yes Album*, when stylistic changes within the band arguably left him out on a limb.

The only weak link – and this is no more than a minor issue on this particular album – is Peter Banks. His gimmicky guitar playing is jazzy and loose, a mix of Pete Townshend and jazz guitarist Wes Montgomery. It is perfectly fine for the material, but it is clear even at this stage that he was not really up to the lofty ambitions of Anderson and Squire.

Despite some remarkably expansive arrangements and some decent original material, particularly 'Survival' – the one true classic here – it is not hard to see why the album failed to make the impression so many had hoped for. There were a myriad of other bands doing things like this in 1969. But the promise of better to come was there.

As for the band themselves, they were a bit disappointed as Banks recounts in his book *Beyond And Before: The Formative Years Of Yes*.

... there was a sense of disappointment because we were smaller – everything sounded so small. In retrospect, it's not a bad album. But everything sounded very compressed, and we did have an engineer telling us to turn down, which really got on our nerves. I think we were a little intimidated by the environment, and the engineer and producer were intimidated by us. Even still, the band seemed to work together well through it all.

'Beyond And Before' (Squire, Clive Bayley)
A single-note guitar riff and a swirl of harmony 'ah's announce the band's first recorded song, written by Squire and Clive Bayley. Bayley was one of the casualties. It's a psychedelic piece, with plenty of Beatles influences, especially in the chord structure and the effects on the middle eight:

Reaching the snow in the days of the cold
Casting a spell out of ice

Groovy, man.

Indeed, one suspects it sounds like Mabel Greer's Toyshop, given The Byrds' influence on the backing vocals. There are no lead vocals – the three vocalists sing the whole piece in harmony.

Squire thumps his way through the song, but also of note is Bruford's drumming – his snare work is much more complex than the norm for such a song, although his fills are a touch overdone. Peter Banks' guitar fills are fine, but no more than that. Nonetheless, it is an impressive start, and the quieter section towards the end shows how polished the band already were at controlling tempo and dynamics, Kaye's organ giving the close an almost neoclassical vibe.

'I See You' (Jim McGuinn, David Crosby)
Banks is far more impressive in his clean jazz style at the start of this fine reworking of such a well-known Byrds song. Anderson gets his first lead vocal proper, with hints of his 'rock' voice, plus a touch of jazz, although the harmonies are still prominent, as is Bruford's excellent cymbal work. It's all played at a fast pace, showing that the band could really rock out when needed.

The guitar/drums (ride cymbal and jazz snare, mainly) duet mid-song – with Banks showing off his ability with the volume knob on his Rickenbacker – could apparently go on for ten minutes in a live setting. Thankfully, we get only a couple of minutes of it here, as there's a reasonable amount of fairly pointless noodling from Banks even in this short version. Once again, Bruford's jazz drumming is spectacular. It's another very solid track with a fine arrangement, and, outside the noodly mid-section, some terrifically good ensemble playing. The close – on 'I love you' – is especially effective.

'Yesterday And Today' (Anderson)
Track three is far quieter, and Anderson gets to show us how good he is with a melody, as the vocal comes straight in. He also double- or possibly triple-tracked his lead vocals, a technique in which he was to develop some skill. The arrangement is delicate, showing a different side to the band, especially as everyone is playing. And there's some effective acoustic guitar work from Banks and some rare but welcome piano from Kaye alongside his ecclesiastical organ. It's all a bit inconsequential and fades a little early, just as Banks is taking a jazzy electric solo.

'Looking Around' (Anderson, Squire)
Clearly slated to be a single, 'Looking Around' is the first attempt at 'the hit', and very fine it is, too. Kaye is upfront with a splendidly bluesy organ riff and some nicely dexterous flourishes, not unlike Keith Emerson. The song itself is also good, mixing lead and harmony vocals beautifully, and the lead vocal melody is very reminiscent of Paul McCartney. Banks is less prominent as Kaye dominates, until a solo before the 'Looking around with my feet on the ground' coda. The reverb on the vocals in this section is also a nice touch. The song really should have been a hit; it's terrifically catchy.

'Harold Land' (Anderson, Squire, Bruford)
Then, all of a sudden, we have progressive rock. The galloping intro to the first track on side two – with Kaye dominant on both organ and piano – sounds rather like *Nursery Cryme*-era Genesis, before straightening out into a more conventional riff-heavy intro. Only the song itself disappoints; it's a rather overwrought 1960s-style anti-war piece, where, for once, the harmony vocals clutter the arrangement rather than enhance it. It's a bold track, and if, in the end, the execution doesn't quite match the ambition, it's an interesting sign of things to come. Bruford's writing credit is probably due to the fact that he came up with the name of the protagonist. 'Harold Land' was the name of a favourite jazzman. This was obviously part of the brief fashion of naming songs after fictitious people during the psychedelic era, typified by 'Eleanor Rigby', and more relevant here (one suspects) 'Arnold Layne' by Pink Floyd, released in 1967. Harold is a more sympathetic character than Arnold and his 'strange hobby' (look it up).

'Harold Land' is an interesting cul-de-sac in Yes music. It's not especially successful, and yet it's recognisably progressive rock, but in a style more reminiscent of Genesis and some of the early 1970s Italian bands than Yes, especially on the return organ-led galloping intro at the end.

'Every Little Thing' (John Lennon, Paul McCartney)
The explosive intro to this Beatles cover epitomises the power of the band, with Banks 'wigging out' somewhat with hints of 'Also Sprach Zarathustra' and Bruford bashing the living daylights out of his kit. The main melody is

introduced before the first vocal, and Banks also slips in a bit of the Beatles mega-hit 'Day Tripper'. One of Banks' traits was to throw in snippets of other songs into his playing, especially during his solos. It's both endearing and a bit irritating in repeated plays.

The harmony vocals on the chorus are sing-along spectacular, and overall, this is a worthy cover, possibly better than the original. The band liked their arrangement enough to recreate it as an encore on the 2004 World Tour, though only Anderson and Squire were present from the original recording.

'Sweetness' (Anderson, Squire, Clive Bayley)
The full band demonstrate that they can do 'delicate' as well as 'powerful' on this slightly sappy ballad, although the arrangement is lovely and the vocals work well as you'd expect, with a nice 'build' towards the chorus. Choosing this over 'Looking Around' as the first single was probably a mistake, as it sank without a trace.

However, it works quite nicely, with effective volume control from Banks, a slightly husky McCartney-esque lead vocal from Anderson and lovely backing vocals.

'Survival' (Anderson)
'Survival' is much loved amongst Yes fans. The intro gives Squire his most obvious bass 'moment' on the album before Kaye's terrific, slightly Eastern-sounding riff takes over as the bass settles into a thunderous groove, punctuated with a lighter rendering of the riff, with some quite cleverly placed reverb. This is a sensational opening, which then gives way to Anderson's delicate verse, accompanied by some equally delicate strumming from Banks, with some lovely acoustic soloing.

The build towards the chorus is beautifully handled, and the simple chorus itself is magical. The final few seconds of the song playfully reprise the intro. A live video version of this song exists from a German TV broadcast, and Kaye is masterful, particularly as his playing has to cover the studio-created transitions in the original. Like many, I wish the band had played this track live more often, though they hinted at it during the version of 'The Fish' played on the 1978/1979 *Tormato* tour.

The *Yesterdays* mix has some odd flanging over the chorus that jars a little. It's not present on the original album version.

Related tracks
'Everydays' (Stephen Stills)
This Stephen Stills song was a live favourite, and it's not hard to see why. The track has a great sense of dynamics, with a perfect midsection to allow organ and guitar soloing. Of the two versions on the Rhino re-master, the so-called 'single version' is the stronger and longer, with great interplay between Banks and Kaye, and a keyboard run from Kaye that is almost Wakeman-like in its

dexterity. The shorter version is also good – it has some great singing from Anderson, and Banks playfully throws a snatch of 'Jesu Joy Of Man's Desiring' into his solo.

'Dear Father' (Anderson, Squire)
Another pop song in the 'Looking Around' mould, the track languished as a *Time And A Word* era B-side, although both the versions on the Rhino remaster are perfectly decent, with version two a little more polished than version one, although its predecessor does have a great deal of energy. Most Yes fans were introduced to this song when it was included on the *Yesterdays* compilation, released in 1974.

'Something's Coming' (Leonard Bernstein, Stephen Sondheim)
The band's expansive arrangement for this classic song from *West Side Story* was the most significant piece in the Yes repertoire circa early 1969 to fail to make it onto a finished album. However, as the two versions on the Rhino remaster show, it certainly deserves some sort of airing. It shows off everything that was good – and not quite so good – about this early version of the band. They certainly knew how to fashion an arrangement and the backing vocals are exceptional in both versions. The later recording is the tighter of the two, though Banks' playful addition of 'Troika' by Prokofiev is perhaps a touch too knowing – I prefer his playing on the earlier, rawer version.

Time And A Word (1970)

Personnel:
Jon Anderson: vocals
Chris Squire: bass, vocals
Peter Banks: guitar, vocals
Bill Bruford: drums
Tony Kaye: organ, piano
David Foster: backing vocals, acoustic guitar
Produced at Advision between December 1969 and February 1970 by Tony Colton
Orchestral arrangements: Tony Cox
Engineer: Eddie Offord
UK release date: July 1970
US release date: November 1970
Highest chart places: UK: 45, US: none
Running time: 39:35

What to do? Despite their growing reputation as a live unit, the response to the band's debut album had been a disappointment to everyone. While it would be an exaggeration to suggest that panic had set in, there was clearly a feeling that something needed to change. What the band might have done was trust in their material and their arrangements since there is little doubt that the songs on *Time And A Word* are an improvement on the previous album. Indeed, at least half the songs on the album were already in the live set, so in theory all the band had to do would be to record them properly.

However, two things happened that were to change everything, both seemingly instigated by Jon Anderson. Firstly, the band decided to use an orchestra to augment the arrangements. This was quite fashionable at the time, as both The Nice and Deep Purple had attempted it with reasonable success. Secondly, Anderson brought in his friend Tony Colton to produce. Colton was the singer of the recently formed Head, Hands and Feet (with Albert Lee on guitar) and had ambitions in the area of production.

While the album sounds markedly better than its predecessor – probably due to the skilled work of a young engineer called Eddie Offord, who would become an important figure on later albums, the orchestral arrangements do 'squeeze' the organ and guitar parts. Yet it is Banks that suffers most. The guitarist argued that Colton's love of blues-based playing did not suit Banks' style, bringing him into conflict with the producer and unsettling the band. So while there is still plenty of guitar on the album, it is not as prominent as it might have been. By contrast, Kaye seems to find the space he needs to make a good impression, a remarkable achievement since the 'job' of a keyboard player in rock music is often to provide orchestral colour.

Otherwise, the album's structure is similar to the first, with two cover versions and six originals that blend styles ranging from pop to near-symphonic rock. The material is more confident, certainly, and in 'Astral Traveller', the band had perhaps found a direction which might work for them when they were to play original material in the future. However, the orchestra, an interesting gimmick though it was, holds the band back from a sound that was already developing and improving.

The band recorded in the new studio at Advision, with Offord engineering. The studio was much better equipped than the one used for the debut, but the orchestra was recorded after the band and Banks felt that they were just doubling the organ and guitar parts. While this does happen a little, Banks's role as an unreliable narrator comes to the fore here. As we will see, the orchestral arrangements, while not perfect, are slightly more imaginative than that.

A concert at the Queen Elizabeth Hall in London with a 20-piece orchestra (20 'pieces' is not a lot and hardly qualifies as an orchestra at all) was a partial success at best, beset by technical issues, and by the late spring of 1970, Banks was out. He had been in continual loggerheads with Colton during the recording of the album, especially when asked to play like Jimmy Page, a musician whose playing Banks hated. In his memoir, Banks states that he was never sure why he was fired from the band, and Anderson has given various comments over the years. Banks admitted he was starting to drift away from the band in terms of his creative contributions, but it was still a big, upsetting shock.

'No Opportunity Necessary, No Experience Needed' (Richie Havens)
The orchestra works well on this opening piece, which mixes a fairly straight rendition of a Richie Havens song – albeit with the usual Yes-style harmonies and some powerful organ – with, well, the theme to the well-known Western film, *The Big Country* (whose author, rather unfortunately, receives no writing credit). It works because the orchestra only interjects during the Western-style section, leaving the band to storm through the main song unencumbered.

Banks is well featured and even throws in a section from 'The Big Country' theme himself.

Steve Howe respected the band prior to his arrival, and as a result, this song has appeared in recent live sets.

'Then' (Anderson)
This is a very strong song written by Anderson – one of the pieces from the album that has stood the test of time. Again, the orchestra – swapping 'licks' with Kaye's organ – works nicely on the verses, but embellishes unnecessarily on the chorus. Kaye is indeed the star here – his solos in the instrumental section are excellent, as is Squire's bass work, while Banks is relegated to rhythm. The breakdown to the quiet section towards the end of the track is nicely done, as is the final 'big band' jazz outro. Nonetheless, this is one of those pieces that didn't really need the orchestra, as the live

versions on the Banks-compiled *Something's Coming* album of BBC sessions illustrate.

'Everydays' (Stephen Stills)
The same can be said of this – the third attempt to record this Stephen Stills song after two versions during the time of the first album. While the piece keeps the bare bones of the arrangement – with Banks' guitar prominent – the orchestral shimmers are superfluous, and we are left longing for one of the earlier versions.

'Sweet Dreams' (Anderson, David Foster)
This was the big single from the album – significantly, recorded without orchestra – and it is rather marvellous. It's straight, catchy pop with a lovely arrangement. Of all the songs from the album, except the title track, this song has had one of the longest live runs. It was played occasionally by the Moraz-era band, and also in almost every show on the 2004 world tour. The track was co-written with Anderson's bandmate from The Warriors, David Foster, who went on to form Badger with Tony Kaye.

'The Prophet' (Anderson, Squire)
A huge neo-classical Hammond introduction from Kaye heralds the return of the orchestra and this splendid mini-epic, with hints of Eastern promise. Banks contributes a lovely, jazzy guitar solo and the song itself, when it arrives, is wonderful, with the orchestra once again providing tasteful embellishment rather than dominating, as it tends to do elsewhere on the album. It's a shame that this piece didn't linger longer in the live set, although Anderson did sing a snatch of it during his Yes medley on his solo *Song Of Seven* tour.

The remaster of *Time And A Word* released by Rhino in 2003 includes a single version of the track, which, somewhat strangely, is almost exactly the same length as the album version (i.e., far too long to be a single). It is a slightly different mix, but doesn't really add or take away anything from the original.

'Clear Days' (Anderson)
This is fragile, pleasant, yet forgettable stuff. Anderson sings a cloyingly romantic tune with a somewhat over-arranged string quartet and (presumably) Kaye's piano. The ending is better than the song. Indeed, the orchestral arrangement would stand alone as a piece of modern classical music. Accompanying the song, it just feels a bit … off.

'Astral Traveller' (Anderson)
Tonally, this great piece is akin to 'Then', but without the orchestra, allowing the entire band – with both Kaye and Banks doing some great work in neo-

classical style – to really let rip. This is the piece that heralds *The Yes Album* to the greatest extent, with Banks experimenting with some different textures and tones in the same way that Howe would do a year later. It's a terrific piece of tuneful, superbly arranged progressive rock, rendered somewhat more '1960s' by the odd effect on the vocals and the overall production quality.

'Time And A Word' (Anderson, Foster)
The title track has been rendered ... er... 'timeless' partly because of its lovely melody and universal sentiment, but also because of Anderson's habit of dusting it off on a regular basis. It was played live on the 1978-79 tour as part of the 'Big Medley' and also in the 1996 *Keys To Ascension* shows, while Anderson included it in his solo medley on the Anderson, Bruford, Wakeman, Howe tour. The Jon Davidson lineup has even played it on occasion to represent the Banks era of the band, even though Banks himself disliked the song. It is a nice tune, although not particularly 'Yes', and suffers from a scratchy guitar introduction, supposedly played by Dave Foster.

The orchestra appears in the repetitive outro, with the band heavily influenced by The Beatles. It works nicely.

'No Opportunity Necessary, No Experience Needed' (Richie Havens)
'Sweet Dreams' (Anderson, David Foster)
The original German pressing of the album included not only 'Dear Father' but also different mixes of these two pieces, which later appeared on the Rhino remaster. Because Banks was the most vocal about these differences, it's possible to be blinkered when assessing them, but actually, these mixes demonstrate what choices mixing engineers had even in 1970.

Yes, there's more Banks lead guitar on the former, but to what purpose? They are a little noodly and not his finest work, and the track is better with these embellishments removed. Also, Kaye's organ is lower in the mix – it's better given more prominence as in the final UK mix.

The same applies to a lesser extent to 'Sweet Dreams', with Banks again reduced in prominence in a noticeably longer version with a deliberately repetitive ending, with more percussion and Anderson attempting McCartney-esque embellishments in the outro. There are more backing vocals that clutter the song a little, so once again this author prefers the final album mix.

Both versions are fascinating, though.

Related Tracks
'Dear Father' (Anderson, Squire)
The final recording of the song, which appeared on the early German versions of the album in place of 'The Prophet' and on the B-side of 'Sweet Dreams', is a more sedate affair than the two recordings that had preceded it, with a rather stately orchestra high in the mix, but it's fine nonetheless. It first saw the light of day in this version on the *Yesterdays* compilation in 1975.

'For Everyone' (Anderson, Squire)
A live version of this song exists from a BBC live set, recorded in March 1970. It feels like a work in progress, with two sections that don't quite fit together. It is a nice Anderson song with a catchy organ riff from Kaye, followed by an early version of 'Disillusion', sung solo by Squire, which later appeared as part of 'Starship Trooper'. It demonstrates that *The Yes Album* wasn't created from scratch in that farmhouse in Devon, making it an interesting glimpse into the past.

Beyond and Before (US title) / Something's Coming (UK title) – the BBC Recordings 1969-1970 (CD) (1997)
Although not all technically 'live' tracks – BBC sessions often allowed overdubs – these interesting recordings were culled (mainly) from BBC sessions during 1969 and 1970 – around the time of the first two albums. Peter Banks curated this double CD set and wrote the liner notes in 1997. Like Banks' entertaining memoir, also called *Beyond And Before*, his writing is a slightly uncomfortable mix of celebration and bitterness. However, the songs themselves are of varying interest and even more variable sound quality. The usual suspects – in terms of tracks – are there and the variations in arrangements are interesting rather than essential. There are a few gems, though. The trio of 'Looking Around' (recorded in August 1969), 'Sweet Dreams' and 'Then' (both recorded for *The Dave Lee Travis Show* in January 1970) are terrific, all played lightning-fast without too many embellishments. The arrangement of 'Sweet Dreams' in particular more than hints at The Beatles at their hardest rocking, with Anderson pulling out all the stops to sound like Paul McCartney. The live set on CD2 (introduced by John Peel) is classy and features 'For Everyone', discussed earlier with *Time And A Word.*

The Yes Album (1971)

Personnel:
Jon Anderson: vocals, percussion
Chris Squire: bass guitar, vocals
Steve Howe: electric and acoustic guitars, Vachalia (Portuguese Guitar), vocals
Tony Kaye: piano, organ, Moog
Bill Bruford: drums, percussion
Produced at Advision in autumn 1970 by Yes and Eddie Offord
Release date: February 1971
Highest chart places: UK: 4, US: 40
Running time: 41:32

The band suffered its first real crisis in the spring of 1970 with the dismissal of Peter Banks. His replacement was Steve Howe, who seems to have been talent-spotted by Squire and Anderson, and it isn't hard to see why. Jazzy and loose, Peter Banks' style fit the band's sound on the first couple of albums perfectly, with its post-psychedelic, proto-progressive hybrid. However, Howe brought something very different to the band. As well as being an unusual and inventive lead player in the rock idiom, he was well-versed in a variety of styles, including the clean jazz of Wes Montgomery and the finger-picking style of Chet Atkins. He was also heavily influenced by classical and flamenco guitar. Although he was always willing to use different sounds and textures – he was an early pioneer of the pedal steel and electric sitar in rock music – his early reliance on his Gibson 175-D hollow-bodied electric guitar gave him a rock sound like no other guitarist.

Howe came in at an awkward time for the band and found himself initially promoting the *Time And A Word* album, even appearing on the American cover and some wacky promotional videos. The band mixed up gigs during the summer of 1970 with intense rehearsals. But when the album was finally released in the UK, it became very clear that this recording was not to be the success they had hoped for, and during their subsequent rehearsals, they were very aware that they were in the 'last chance saloon' with their label Atlantic. Indeed, it appears that they were to be dropped but that their main supporter at the label, Phil Carson, bailed them out at the last minute.

Yes, fans still speculate about what might have happened in that house in Devon while they were working on the new material. Was it desperation that pushed them to the new level they reached in the composition of this album, or was it that extra spark of energy that Howe provided?

What emerged from their time in the West Country was such a great leap forward – an evolutionary jump to rival the Cambrian explosion – that, as a Yes fan, it almost boggles the mind. All of the album – with the exception of 'A Venture' – remains in the band's main repertoire to this day. The tracks remain band and fan favourites, endlessly re-interpreted (with respect, of course) by whichever incarnation happens to exist at the time.

Three things seem to have happened when looking at the album as a whole:

Firstly, the band were hugely confident as a unit, some of which will have been down to natural progression resulting from the two years they had been playing together. However, they also had the foresight not to rely on cover versions to fill out albums as they had previously. They were determined to forge their own path in whatever direction it took them.

Secondly, there is little doubt that Steve Howe's presence gave them a genuine shot in the arm. Peter Banks was a talented musician, but Howe came in brimming with ideas and also possibilities. Much mimicked and copied in later years, it would simply not have been possible for another musician to bring in such a broad range of influences. Rock musicians these days have so much more actual rock history to fall back on. Howe drew inspiration from Jimi Hendrix and Eric Clapton, of course, but he was also listening to the blues, jazz, bluegrass and even classical guitar music. He had so much more colour to draw upon than most rock guitarists.

Finally, when we listen to *The Yes Album* now, we do not hear the 1960s; we hear modernity. The first two albums were well recorded for their time; indeed, the band recorded *The Yes Album* at the same studio (Advision) as *Time And A Word* and with the same engineer, Eddie Offord. Yet *The Yes Album* sounds completely different. It has an almost antiseptic clarity. Gone is that bass-y boom that characterised much of the recording of the late 1960s. Instead, we have an album where each instrument stands alone in the mix, clear and intimate. The vocals, for instance, are recorded with far less reverb than previously, and sit high in the mix. Tony Kaye's organ is also nakedly prominent. In the course of little more than six months, the band had left the 1960s and joined 'the modern era'.

Released in February 1971, the album was a commercial success in the UK, reaching number four, and a minor one in the US. Chris Squire sometimes suggested in interviews that the album charted so well due to a postal strike in Britain during early 1971, which meant that when the album was first released, chart returns could only be counted from London-based record stores, where Yes had a strong following. But then again, most rock bands need a little dose of luck occasionally, so it is hard to begrudge them a little accidental leg up, whether there is truth in the story or not.

The Yes Album is innovative and groundbreaking, and yet I rarely play it. While I recognise how hugely important it is in the Yes story, the pieces on it have had so many superb live interpretations over the years that the originals now seem a little naive. Additionally, so deft is the exuberant playing of Howe throughout the album that Tony Kaye – often a dexterous player in the past – seems a little out of place, even obvious at times, particularly with his organ arrangements. It is not hard to see why this was the next area the band felt they needed to improve.

Although now seen as a ground-breaking progressive rock record, playing it again, it is definitely a transitional album. While he has since become a poster boy for avoiding clichés in guitar playing, on his first album with the band, Steve Howe actually plays a fair amount of blues-based licks, and had Kaye stayed, it is quite possible that the band might have developed into a harder-edged outfit. But in the end, with Rick Wakeman's arrival, a more progressive path was chosen.

'Yours Is No Disgrace' (Anderson, Squire, Howe, Kaye, Bruford)
As a statement of intent, it doesn't get much better than this. The 'new' Yes is presented here, fully formed and in all its glory in a song that is clearly – and famously – about the Vietnam War. Yet it also shows Anderson playing with words and phrases; much of his meaning is veiled in obscurity. It shows the author moving towards a more impressionistic turn of phrase.

Meanwhile, the sound is pristine – dry, almost. Each instrument can be heard, crystal clear without being buried in unnecessary reverb. The initial unison riff gives way to big Hammond organ chords and the first vocal section. One of the important features of this track is the lack of a 'lead' vocal for most of the song – it's a three-part harmony for almost all the verses, with Howe soloing between phrases. This is terrific, stirring stuff, with Howe and indeed Bruford on fire. This section also features the first use of a Moog synthesizer on a Yes album, playing the melody line. The next section is the same vocal line, but this time – brilliantly – sung over a simple, mostly ascending bass line. Then we're back into a repeat of the opening salvo before an extended instrumental section, beginning with some percussive guitar work before a lengthy and innovative solo from Howe – relatively short here, but extended for several minutes at live shows. In fact, it's not a single solo, but two overlapping ones, with very different voicings. Then, at last, there's a lead vocal – Anderson singing over a simple bass and acoustic guitar pattern – before a return to the main verse played by the full band to a close.

'Yours Is No Disgrace' is nine minutes and 40 seconds of real innovation. The band had never tried anything as bold in its construction as this, and it immediately demonstrated that Howe was a genuine and prodigious talent. With Eddie Offord making each instrument sound ... real ... it is no wonder that the piece has lasted so well, regularly part of the live set almost 50 years later.

As the *Yessongs* version shows, the piece became a jumping-off point for Howe to improvise boldly. Indeed, the version on that live album is interesting as it's clear that Howe's solo could go on for as long as he wanted, and you can hear him trying things – not all of which come off – but it must have been thrilling to be in the room as he improvised.

'Clap' (Howe)
Forever known as 'The Clap' due to Anderson's mischievous mistitling during his introduction to this live recording, this remains Howe's most famous solo guitar piece, written in celebration of the birth of his first son Dylan. It has

been performed thousands of times at live shows, sometimes played dead straight or often rearranged with other acoustic pieces. It remains the centrepiece of Howe's acoustic set – usually two tracks long – to this day.

'Clap' is a lovely Chet Atkins-influenced piece with hints of 'Classical Gas' (by US guitarist Mason Williams) in its chord structure. However, it's hard to believe it is worthy of so much attention; after all, it's a splendid – but hardly consequential – little piece. It shows what resonance this album has with Yes's fan base that even a 'throwaway' track like this can resonate down through the decades.

A studio version of it can be found on the Steven Wilson remix version of the album, which also includes a section from 'Mood For A Day'. It's not as good – there are a couple of missed notes and a rather buzzy string. This live version was recorded at the Lyceum in London on 17 July 1970 – one of Howe's first gigs with the band.

'Starship Trooper (Life Seeker/Disillusion/Würm)' (Anderson, Squire, Howe)

While 'Yours Is No Disgrace' was almost perfect 'right out of the box', 'Starship Trooper' feels a touch sterile in its studio incarnation; so many wonderful live versions have there been over the years. Rather than the sophisticated layering of sections we have in the opening track, here we have three parts – one after the other. However, the pieces still work nicely together, and the band, across 60 years, have never really altered them in the thousands of live arrangements.

The opening section – 'Life Seeker' – written by Anderson, is something he might have written during the *Time And A Word* era, but here the arrangement is much more confident and bolder. Again, Kaye plays some Moog for colour, and his Hammond and Howe's guitar complement each other nicely.

Howe's frantically-picked acoustic guitar introduces 'Disillusion', written by Squire, originally to be found as part of a song, 'For Everyone', a piece from the Banks era that was later abandoned. There's a live version on the *Beyond And Before* compilation of live and session tracks compiled by Banks in 1997. In that version, it's sung by Squire. However, on *The Yes Album,* it's sung by Anderson with a harmony vocal from its author. The close harmony vocal section reintroduces 'Life Seeker' briefly, before the 'Würm' section, which is basically a three-chord sequence repeated with embellishments by the band, a gradual increase in activity from Bruford and a guitar solo – again, a duet on both sides of the stereo – from Howe to the fade-out.

Kaye's own organ embellishments in the 'Würm' section on the album version seem tame, given what we now know about subsequent live renderings, but presumably, it was what he was asked to do at the time, with the limelight going once again to Howe. All the 'markers' we know from live renditions are there on the studio version, including Squire's dainty bass figure just before the guitar solos. The band will have known at the time that the potential for this track as a live piece was huge, but the nine-minute song has grown to almost 15 minutes in some cases.

Given its usual place as an encore, there have been many arrangement embellishments over the years, including two fabulous Wakeman Minimoog solos on the spectacular *Tormato* tour version, still only available as a bootleg. Indeed, the 'Würm' section can include bass, synthesizer or organ solos before the main guitar solo, or even a duet between Moog and guitar. Although not used as often as 'Roundabout' as a final encore, it never fails to bring the house down.

'I've Seen All Good People (Your Move/All Good People)'
(Anderson, Squire)
If side one of the album defined Yes's new style of progressive rock, then the first track on side two was to show off a newfound confidence in songwriting and just a hint of the good-time rock that, as a band, they were beginning to move away from. Again, this famous track has been played at the majority of live performances since, although less so outside the Anderson era.

'Your Move' is possibly Anderson's finest 'conventional' song, but it could only have been written in the era it was, as the optimism of the 1960s gave way to the rather more cynical 1970s. Its metaphor for human relationships, based on the movement of chess pieces, is well done, as it could easily have been overbearing, and the backing vocals are beautifully arranged. So too are Colin Goldring's recorders – a rare example of a guest musician playing on a Yes album in the early years. Howe plays an instrument misidentified as the Portuguese 12-stringed Vachalia for many years. In fact, it's a laud, a Spanish instrument. He also played it on 'Wonderous Stories' on *Going For The One*. The insertion of John Lennon's famous 'All We Are Saying Is Give Peace A Chance' line as a counterpoint to the main melody could only have worked in the early 1970s. Indeed, any time after the *Fragile* era, and it might have seemed trite. The final surge at the end of the track is followed by an uncomfortable silence in this studio version, leading into the 'All Good People' section written by Squire.

This is pretty much blues rock – a repetitive vocal line over a simple chord progression, with Howe soloing on his trusty Gibson ES-175. While this section works really well as a clap/dance-along piece at live shows, here it feels sterile and a little uncomfortable; well played though it is.

'A Venture' (Anderson)
This brief track has always been considered the other 'throwaway' piece on the album, but it works very nicely as a palette cleanser before the big finish of 'Perpetual Change'. Tonally, it is not dissimilar to the much better-known 'Long Distance Runaround', with a jaunty, off-beat arrangement, some nice (if unspectacular) piano work from Kaye and some very good lead guitar work

from Howe. The Steven Wilson remix has an extended version of the track, which is excellent. In it, the song continues into a rather decent jam that would have worked well on the album, but the fade-out is understandable given the time constraints of a vinyl side. The band had bigger fish to fry!

The song has rarely been played live, although Howe has always expressed a liking for it, and even played it during his guest appearances with the Yes tribute band, Fragile. It was, of course, played when the band played *The Yes Album* in its entirety during their 'single album' shows.

'Perpetual Change' (Anderson, Squire)

And so to the big finish. 'Perpetual Change' straddles the line between possible directions for the band. Were they to follow a classic/hard rock path or something a little more neo-classical? It begins with a unison riff played by guitar and piano, and Howe's playing, again, is more blues-oriented than it was to be on later albums. The softer main verse has some good piano work from Kaye, with Howe playing guitar harmonics. Strangely enough, Kaye's piano playing is more impressive than his organ work on *The Yes Album*, and the 'You'll See Perpetual Change' 'hook' has a real feeling of rhythm and blues. There's a sudden segue into a much jazzier passage, featuring a hugely impressive and fluid solo from Howe, before the uber-prog of the quirky guitar/organ/bass/drums figure, gradually moving to the left of the stereo, before another full band arrangement seeps in from the right playing something completely different until meeting in the middle on a swirl of Moog synthesizer, a return to the main chorus and a big finish to the final fade out.

This is innovative stuff. I can't think of another example of this technique in recorded rock music. Indeed, the section where there are effectively two bands playing presents a challenge to the band when arranging as a live piece, but they accomplished it, and once again, it has become a staple, if not exactly a constant, of the live set. It is sometimes played as an opener, and like 'Yours Is No Disgrace' can – and has – been extended to allow longer solos. It's one of Trevor Rabin's favourite Yes pieces from other incarnations of the band, so has been regularly played by lineups that have included him.

Fragile (1971)

Personnel:
Jon Anderson: vocals
Bill Bruford: drums and percussion
Steve Howe: electric and acoustic guitars, vocals
Chris Squire: bass guitars and vocals
Rick Wakeman: organ, grand piano, electric piano, harpsichord, Mellotron, synthesizer
Produced at Advision in September 1971 by Yes and Eddie Offord
Engineered by Eddie Offord, assisted by Gary Martin
UK release date: December 1971
US release date: January 1972
Highest chart places: UK: 7, US: 4
Running time: 41:10

Fragile saw another lineup change, and a crucial one at that, with Tony Kaye replaced by Strawbs (and session) keyboard player Rick Wakeman. Kaye had (arguably) begun to sound out of his depth on *The Yes Album*, and while it does actually contain a fair amount of synthesizer and piano, his performance was still largely organ-based. There is also a suggestion of a personality clash between the hard-partying Kaye and the more reserved Howe. But in the end, Squire and Anderson wanted something a little more orchestral and flamboyant in the Keith Emerson mode, and Wakeman, who had already played Mellotron on David Bowie's 'Space Oddity' as early as 1969, seemed perfect. His virtuosity was somewhat misplaced and underutilised in his current band, The Strawbs, as a listen to their excellent *Just A Collection Of Antiques And Curios* live album testifies.

Wakeman himself had a decision to make. Having just played piano on David Bowie's *Hunky Dory,* which itself was not to be a success until the release of *Ziggy Stardust* the following year, he'd been asked to join the ambitious singer's band, The Spiders From Mars. Wakeman chose Yes.

The new lineup began rehearsing immediately after Kaye's departure and worked up new material for an album that their label, Atlantic, and the band hoped would capitalise quickly on the considerable success of *The Yes Album*. The material was very strong, but only one problem remained. There wasn't enough of it. As a result, each member of the group contributed a solo track with varying degrees of success.

Howe's 'Mood For A Day', for instance, is a delightful classical piece, in contrast to the country pickin' of 'Clap', while Squire and Anderson's pieces also have a lot of charm. Wakeman's 'Cans And Brahms' is hampered by his contract with A&M Records, which prevented him from contributing a self-penned piece, and Bruford's track feels a little pointless. However, the band-created pieces are astonishing. In particular, Wakeman's parts on this (and *Close To The Edge*) are his most imaginative and integrated contributions to the Yes catalogue. Alongside his florid virtuosity and undoubted talents with multiple keyboards, his classical training enhanced the band's ability to transition between sections within a single track. All four of the full-band pieces have remained in the band's live set (more on than off) since the album was released. Yet the solo tracks blight the album just a little. Another month spent on the record might have removed the need for these pieces and produced the classic that was not to arrive for a few months with *Close To The Edge*.

This was the first Yes album to make use of the skills of Roger Dean, an elegant and amiable Englishman whose unique fantasy paintings have become so synonymous with the band's music. Note that the band's famous snake-like logo had not yet arrived, but the otherworldly nature of the artwork fitted perfectly with the ambiguous nature of Anderson's lyrics.

The vinyl version of the album came complete with a gatefold sleeve and a booklet, which were reproduced in miniature on the 2016 Definitive Edition CD. Clearly, neither the band nor Atlantic were taking any chances.

'Roundabout' (Anderson, Howe)

This iconic rocker remains the perfect calling card to the 'classic' version of the band. Howe's classical guitar introduction leads into the main song, which emphasises Squire's mobile bass and Wakeman's terrific organ arpeggios. It is possible to imagine Kaye playing this, but not with quite such effortless fluidity. Bruford's cymbal work – as usual – is first-rate on the middle part of the track, which also includes some unusual organ chords that Kaye could not have contributed, plus the first of the characteristic vocal harmony sections so beloved of the band. Listen out, too, for the casual virtuosity of Wakeman's playing low in the mix over the acoustic guitar reprise before the first Mellotron appearance on a Yes album, and that great organ/guitar dual before the final reprise of the main theme.

The track lays out the album's sound palette, both instrumentally and tonally. The 1960s have gone entirely by this point, and any of the clean sterility that might have slightly blighted *The Yes Album* has been replaced by a warm, natural and – it has to be said – even more modern sound. If you are reading this, Eddie Offord, take a bow.

Despite some impressionistic phraseology, 'Roundabout' is essentially a love song. This is Anderson on the road, playing music to 'the children' but looking forward to seeing his love. That's pretty much it. 'Mountains come out of the sky' is relatively literal, referring to the impression of seeing mountains rearing out of the fog on a love drive to a gig.

This most perfect of up-tempo Yes pieces has developed a life of its own, of course. An edited version of the song was a big – and unexpected – hit single in the US, which – in turn – has led to it being played as an encore in almost every Yes show since. Sometimes – particularly when there is another guitarist alongside Howe (e.g., Trevor Rabin or Billy Sherwood) playing in the band – a full version has been performed with Howe playing acoustic for the first couple of minutes of the track. At other times, various edits have been used – usually to preserve that full-tilt 'encore' vibe. On the 2004 world tour, the song was relegated to the acoustic section and played – entertainingly – as a shuffle. There are various alternative versions on the 2003 Rhino re-master and 2016 Definitive Edition (including the US single edit, which I had never heard before), and countless live versions, but the original on *Fragile* still takes some beating.

'Cans And Brahms' (Brahms Arr: Wakeman)
This is a slight piece – albeit a pleasant listen – and had it not been placed on such a famous album, it would never have warranted the attention it still gets to this day. Indeed, it has a bit of a 'Switched On Bach' feel to it, which may be intentional. However, as a calling card for Wakeman's ability, it does say a couple of things.

Firstly: 'The classics are important to me'. Secondly: 'Look at how many keyboards I have'. Both these may seem obvious to us, 55-years on, but given that most keyboard players were still rhythm and blues organists at the time, it sends an important message to the Yes-buying public. When the band toured playing *Fragile* in its entirety in 2015, the track – played by Geoff Downes – seemed completely pointless.

'We Have Heaven' (Anderson)

Tell the Moondog, tell the March hare.

Originally planned as an *a capella* piece, this Anderson solo track has a bit more about it than Wakeman's, with Anderson building up layered vocals over a very basic acoustic guitar, bass and drums backing. A longer version and an *a capella* mix can be found on the Steven Wilson Definitive Version Blu-ray. The song – like Wakeman's track, rather short – foreshadows Anderson's great solo album *Olias Of Sunhillow* in 1976 with its joyous tone and beautifully-crafted backing vocals. Footsteps – panning nicely over the stereo – lead into the next piece, which is ...

'South Side Of The Sky' (Anderson, Squire)
This full-band track is the first to use strong non-musical atmospherics on a Yes album, with rolls of thunder and swirls of wind introducing us to another rocker with Howe soloing hard and Anderson's double-tracked vocals wailing over a complex and powerful riff played by guitar, bass and organ in unison at times.

After this hard-rocking section, the piece takes an unexpected turn with its neo-classical piano solo – again, the first of its type on a Yes album– and the following vocal section with Chris Squire dominant (rather than Anderson) and guitar almost completely absent. This is wonderfully done and lifts the track to something very unusual. Bruford gets the chance to use his jazz chops here, before a reprise of the hard rock section and a further swirl of wind close the track and, indeed, the first side of the album. There's a fantastic feeling of 'space' on this track. I love, for instance, the way that the final low piano note of Wakeman's solo section is allowed to resonate and swirl across the stereo before the next section. It's spectacular and confident stuff.

This great track was tried out as a live piece on the *Fragile* tour but dropped quickly, as it didn't seem to gel. It may simply have been that the technology, particularly the live sonic reproduction of the grand piano, so critical to the piece, just did not work at the time. However, it was attempted successfully in 2003, when digital samples had made reproduction of a grand piano in a live rock setting much easier. It seemed to work so well that it has been part of many live sets since. Played by the band of 2003-4, which included Howe and Wakeman, it was extended to feature a thrilling guitar/ Minimoog duel.

'Five Per Cent For Nothing' (Bruford)
Bruford's 35-second instrumental track – played by the whole band – is somewhat throwaway due to its brevity. So seeing the band, in late middle age, have to play this piece in a live setting because of a commitment to playing the complete album is a little odd. The title refers to the deal that Roy Flynn – the band's first manager – negotiated on his way out. Bruford, who didn't actually come up with the title, has more recently suggested that his somewhat acerbic song title was a little unkind in retrospect, especially in light of Flynn's death in 2026.

'Long Distance Runaround' (Anderson)
Considering its relative fame in the catalogue, this lively but short piece feels rather slight in the cold light of day. Indeed, as a live track, it has tended to work as a full-band introduction to the same piece as it does on the album, Chris Squire's solo track 'The Fish'. It remains good fun, though, an early example of the way that Howe and Wakeman could feature in a track without getting in each other's way, usually playing in harmony – Howe on electric guitar, Wakeman on electric piano, then acoustic piano for the verses. Squire's wandering bass and Bruford's inventive snare work are both excellent, creating a stabbing arrangement to complement Anderson's tuneful song melody.

'The Fish (Schindleria Praematurus)' (Squire)
Often misrepresented as a bass solo, probably due to its use as a stepping-off point for a solo in live concerts, this inventive piece, mainly created by overdubbed bass guitars, actually includes some nice electric guitar and mallet percussion interjections, as well as the repeated vocal refrain just

before the fade-out. Unlike some of the live solos it inspired, the track also gets to the point quite quickly. Overall, it's an inventive use of the instrument and does bear repeated listening, unlike Bruford and Wakeman's solo pieces on this same album.

'Mood For A Day' (Howe)
Howe's classical guitar track really is a solo piece, showing off his growing maturity as a player and composer. The performance is not perfect, but it is spontaneous and dynamic, beautifully recorded with great warmth. Only 'Clap' retains more resonance with Yes fans; 'Mood For A Day' is played in a live setting much less regularly.

'Heart Of The Sunrise' (Anderson, Squire, Bruford)
Despite the great pieces that Yes had already committed to vinyl, not least 'Roundabout', which opens this album, 'Heart Of The Sunrise' feels, to me, like the first bona fide Yes masterpiece. It is the first true representation of what the mature Yes would be capable of. It is a seemingly effortless combination of virtuosity, extreme dynamics and structure over its 11 or so minutes.

The opening riff – carried by guitar and organ before the famous bass section, which builds in intensity aide by the ascending Mellotron chords that accompany it and Bruford's masterful drumming There's nothing particularly complex about Squire's playing here; he's varying a simple riff, yet it's the building of tension that works so well.

The song then breaks down into the first vocal section – the band is tentative at first, before introducing themes that will later appear in more powerful form, delicately played here. Listen to the subtle keyboards in this section, a touch of Moog here, a snatch of piano there, and then 'sharp, distance ' brings us to the first peak. The next instrumental section combines the main riff with a counterbalancing, staccato section, with Moog again dominant. The effortless way that Squire and Bruford switch between these two repeating sections is remarkable.

Next, we are into the piano-led section – 'straight light moving and removing' – this is a new riff entirely, taken up by the whole band with Anderson now double-tracked and Wakeman switching between piano and organ, building to the final Mellotron swirl and the powerful, triumphant final vocal section: 'Love comes to you, then after'. On the BBC *Sounding Out* documentary, first broadcast in 1972, a youthful Wakeman admits to struggling with this sharp transition in early live performances.

To a 16-year-old author hearing this for the first time in 1978, this was life-changing music. It still sends shivers down my spine now. The piece ends playfully with an opening door and a return to 'We Have Heaven' – as if it continues forever in a room somewhere. You just need to open the right door ...

'Heart Of The Sunrise' has, of course, been played live many times over the years, usually in an arrangement close to the original. As a mid-set showstopper, it is only challenged by 'And You And I'. Even in his final live shows with the band, Squire – ever the showman – made the most of his bass solo.

Related Tracks

'Show Me' (Anderson)

I am placing this track here because, according to Anderson's introduction to the song on the *New Director's Cut* DVD, he found it on an old cassette from this era. It is a sweet, folky ditty that was played on the 2003-4 tours, so can only be found on the *Songs From Tsongas* live CD set, as an interlude on the 2003 tour (with Wakeman) and in the acoustic set in 2004 (and on the *Yes Acoustic* DVD) with a slightly different arrangement.

'America' (Simon)

A remnant from the covers band of 1968-69, the group first recorded a shorter version of their – somewhat expansive – ten-minute arrangement of this Simon and Garfunkel song with Kaye on organ before definitively re-recording it – with Wakeman on organ, Mellotron and electric piano – for an Atlantic Records compilation in 1971. An earlier, inferior live version can be found on the *Word Is Live* album. The final, guitar-dominated arrangement from 1971 features only parts of the original Paul Simon song, and somewhat sidelines Wakeman, who, according to Howe, wasn't especially interested in the recording, although as a backup player his contributions are still good.

It has reared its head occasionally in live sets over the years – most notably in 1996 for *The Keys To Ascension* live shows and in 2008 on the *Open Your Eyes* tour.

'All Fighters Past' (precise authorship unknown)

Discovered by remix maestro Steven Wilson on the master tapes from this era and to be found only on the Blu-ray in his reissue of *Fragile*, this full-band piece was understandably dropped, with both tune and lyrics recycled for 'The Revealing Science Of God' two years later.

Close To The Edge (1972)

Personnel:
Jon Anderson: vocals
Bill Bruford: percussion
Steve Howe: guitars, vocals
Chris Squire: bass, vocals
Rick Wakeman: keyboards
Produced at Advision between February and June 1972 by Yes and Eddie Offord.
Tapes: Mike Dunne
Co-ordinator: Brian Lane
Released: September 1972
Highest chart places: UK: 4, US: 5
Running time: 37:51

And so to *Close To The Edge*. This astonishing piece of work is one of the most celebrated albums of the progressive rock era, and one wonders what to say about an album that has been so widely discussed, so analysed and so loved over the years. Musicologist Edward Macan examined the side-long title track in detail in his *Rocking The Classics* book, while journalist Will Romano dedicated an entire book to the album in 2017 with his *Close To The Edge: How Yes's Masterpiece Defined Progressive Rock*. What needs to be said? Well, let me give it a go...

Fragile, for all its success, was based around a relatively small amount of band-created material, essentially three long pieces in 'Roundabout', 'South Side Of The Sky' and 'Heart Of The Sunrise'. The album had been produced in something of a hurry to meet demand, especially in the UK, but had gone on to reach markets the band could only have dreamed about. Now the time had come to work on a new band album. The bulk of the new material was rehearsed during the spring of 1972 at the Una Billings School of Dance in Shepherd's Bush before transitioning into recording time at Advision in June, although it is clear that by the time they went into Advision with Eddie Offord, they were still writing material, leading to a somewhat tortuous, argumentative process.

In his autobiography, Bill Bruford refers to the band at the time as being 'painfully democratic', with every decision during the making of the album argued over endlessly. The band had complete creative freedom, and they exercised it, with every bar and every instrumental choice agonised over endlessly.

Bruford hated the process, but with Yes in one of those rare states where every member had equal status, this is how the band operated. On this occasion, whether by fluke, genius or a combination of both, it worked. It has often been noted that the album's back cover features six photographs, all of equal size and status. There is one shot of each member of the band, plus Eddie Offord. The message is clear: 'There are six of us in the band now.'

Close To The Edge is, arguably, progressive rock's defining statement. It is 38 minutes of power, tenderness and passion. It is, by turns, atonal and supremely melodic; it is powerful and gentle, both intensely meaningful and, at the same time, completely and dazzlingly meaningless. It contains surprises and even some mistakes, but not one second of filler. The music drips with atmosphere, achieved not just by the players' musicianship but by clever transitions and the use of reverb, effects and microphone positioning. Furthermore, each musician is at the top of his game. The creativity on display is astonishing, yet the process was too much for Bruford, who moved on to join King Crimson shortly after the completion of the album.

'Close To The Edge (The Solid Time Of Change/Total Mass Retain/I Get Up, I Get Down/Seasons Of Man)' (Anderson, Howe)
Having mastered ten-minute tracks on the previous two albums, Yes decided to attempt a single, side-long piece of music, and right out of the traps, they nailed it. They were not the only band to consider this idea at the time; at the same time that Yes exited Una Billings School of Dance to go to Advision, Genesis were setting up in the same location to rehearse *Foxtrot,* which was to have its own side-long piece, 'Suppers Ready'. Indeed, given the classical composers that the band – particularly Anderson – were listening to, such as Sibelius, Mahler and Stravinsky, who often produced complex movements and suites that clocked in at around a side of vinyl, it must have seemed a natural – if ambitious – continuation of the band's growth.

From the start of the track, it is made very clear that we are entering a very special 'world'. A mixture of synthesizer birdsong and keyboard effects leads us into the opening section, perhaps the most controversial sequence on the album as it is quite atonal, with Howe's guitar soloing over a discordant, almost chaotic pattern, with Wakeman's organ part seemingly unrelated to what the rest of the band are playing, punctuated by Anderson's multi-tracked 'aaaahhhs'. As a solo section in the middle of a piece, this opening salvo would not be controversial, but as the opening of a track, it is provocative. Is it *all* going to be like this?

No, as it turns out, because, at three minutes, the opening section resolves itself with more massed voices, and segues into the superb main theme, played on guitar, which is then varied with a relatively conventional progressive arrangement with Wakeman continuing on organ. The first vocal section, 'A seasoned witch could call you...' begins, with Squire's bass swooping in and out and Howe accompanying on electric sitar. Cleverly, Anderson had been the only backing vocalist to that point, but at the 'chorus' – 'down at the edge, round by the corner' – we also hear Squire and Howe, before heading straight into a simpler section, with percussive keyboards, and a re-iteration of the chorus. 'Total Mass Retain' is largely a re-iteration of the first section, but Anderson's voice changes here – a touch more urgent and presented with a touch less reverb. Squire and Bruford are astonishing –

locked together but landing their blows in unexpected, almost random patterns. Wakeman punctuates the verses with alternate sections of Mellotron and Moog. After 'I get up, I get down', a key change heralds an instrumental section with bass and electric sitar playing one melody, while an organ plays a variation of the main theme.

It's all change for the third section, 'I Get Up, I Get Down'. No longer are we in a forest; we are now deep underground, the mood set by a Mellotron, drenched in reverb, some guitar low in the mix and bass Moog patterns. We hear the drip of water, placing us in a huge cave, the band lost in its vastness.

This is resolved by a simple chord pattern, played on organ, followed by two vocal melodies, the first 'in her white lace...' sung by Howe and Squire, and the counterpoint by Anderson of 'I get up, I get down'. This is simply beautiful, a remarkable piece of construction, with Squire's backing vocals at their very best. The climax introduces Wakeman's massive-sounding church organ – recorded remotely at St. Giles-Without-Cripplegate Church in London, and then spliced in by Offord – which, after a solo section, is then accompanied by another chorus of 'I get up, I get down' with Anderson alone this time. With the organ still playing, we build to a climax via a series of powerful Minimoog runs, and then three Moog 'chimes' doubled by percussion, and the band thumps back in for the closing 'Seasons Of Man' section. Moog now plays a variation on the main theme, leading into 'that' famed Hammond organ solo. This is high-octane stuff, with the band's accompaniment daring and imaginative.

Wakeman makes a couple of little mistakes in the solo – there's a tiny bum note at 15.51, for instance (have a listen) – but the take will have been used for its energy, no doubt. It is spine-tingling, air-keyboard-inducing stuff. The final section reiterates the opening verses, but with Squire and Bruford varying their parts with great verve before the final, climactic reprise of the chorus. Wakeman now plays Mellotron and piano rather than organ, and we fade away back into the chorus of birds, leaving the listener breathless. It's interesting how faithful Wakeman's solo is on the *Yessongs* movie. The mistake is ironed out, though.

Anderson and Howe's lyrics remain about as open to interpretation as any of Yes' pieces. We have many allusions to what may be the 'river of life' and also the change and evolution of mankind, but I will leave others to attempt better interpretations, as several have. What is most thrilling here is the way themes are introduced and endlessly varied in so many exciting ways. Wakeman's compositional training seems to have been important, glueing the arrangements together in a far more sophisticated way than the band had attempted before. It is 18 minutes and 42 seconds long, and every second counts.

Although not as obvious a 'shoe-in' for the setlist as (say) 'And You And I', the band have played 'Close To The Edge' live hundreds of times over the years, and while several keyboard players have played it in addition to

Wakeman – Moraz, Downes, Khoroshev and even session man Tom Brislin on the *Symphonic* tour, for instance – Howe has played the guitar on every live version to date. Unlike 'And You And I', it has never been played with Rabin in the band. As a closely arranged piece of music, there have been relatively few attempts to alter the instrumentation, although Alan White changed the drum part a fair amount when he first played it in 1972.

Given that the church organ section could not be reproduced live until the 1990s, the band have always accentuated this section with percussion and bass to add drama. The organ solo is an opportunity for improvisation, but otherwise, the band have always stuck pretty close to the original recording, so there are many versions to choose from – of varying quality, tempo and recording skill, of course – but only differing slightly in their basic arrangement.

'And You And I (Cord Of Life/Eclipse/The Preacher, The Teacher/ Apocalypse)' (Anderson, Bruford, Howe, Squire)

After the intensity of the title track (or 'side one'), we mellow out for a while with this ten-minute masterpiece. 'And You And I' is one of only three pieces ('Roundabout' and 'I've Seen All Good People' are the other two) deemed necessary to play at almost every live show – until the end of the Anderson era, at least.

Howe plays a few harmonics, says 'ok' and we begin. This is a confident and intimate start, and worth noting. Many songs, throughout the ages, begin with a count-in or studio chatter, but nobody does it quite like this.

The piece has a simple and effective opening, a little guitar figure – beautifully recorded (you can hear the natural reverb in the room), before the gentle bass guitar and bass drum pulse bring in Howe's strummed riff. There's a triangle in there, too, leading to Wakeman's famous Minimoog line, which introduces Anderson's first vocal. Howe's guitar provides a counterpoint, followed by the full band, and the first statement of the 'chorus' such as it is, and a big build to the fantastic 'Eclipse' section. This was written by Bruford and Squire, but dominated by the superb combination of Mellotron and Moog playing in unison. It delivers a huge emotional punch, augmented by Howe's guitar and Anderson's emotion-drenched lead vocal.

We return to Howe's tentative 12-string guitar figure, but this time it introduces a picked, country-style pattern in 'The Preacher, The Teacher' that suggests bluegrass, with Anderson's vocal delivered almost without reverb at all as a contrast to 'Eclipse', in what is the most 'conventional' section of the piece.

Squire's bass re-enters with Howe now playing rhythm guitar and Wakeman vamping on Fender Rhodes piano before he then repeats the Moog line from earlier. This time, it's extended into a solo, a final vocal section, a return to the 'Eclipse' theme and a descending grand piano line, before the reiteration of the chorus and the faintest Moog note ascending in pitch into infinity...

To say this piece 'brings the house down' at live shows would be an understatement. Usually played mid-set (or occasionally before an interval), it is a cathartic moment for band and audience. However, it has had plenty of arrangement tweaks over the decades. In the years before acoustic instruments were usable in full-band settings, the band would open with the dramatic 'Eclipse' section before going straight into the initial strummed riff, usually played on a 12-string electric. More recent performances, however, have returned to the gentle tone of the studio version. From early live performances onwards, Howe doubled Wakeman's keyboards in the 'Eclipse' section on pedal steel, with some embellishments, as this emphasis works better in a live setting. Squire added harmonica to the 'Preacher, Teacher' section, presumably to complement the country/bluegrass style. Trevor Rabin always plays his parts with great respect to Howe's originals when performing this piece.

'Siberian Khatru' (Anderson, Howe, Wakeman)
Given the intricacy and intensity of the first 29 minutes of the album, it is completely understandable that the band should want to rock out to close the record. But this is Yes – there is always a twist in the tale. Howe opens things up with an electric guitar figure followed by the main riff – played by Wakeman, combining organ and Mellotron. Bruford's drumming seems simple, yet as usual, he places accents where you least expect them, leading into the main verse sung by a reverb-drenched Anderson, with Bruford's perky tambourine high in the mix and Wakeman playing some 'rock 'n' roll' Hammond.

There's a nice moment of tension, with bass, guitar and snare only marking time, before the launch into the next verse. Howe's electric sitar figure leads into a completely unexpected harpsichord solo – beautifully played, too – accompanied, delightfully, by Squire's bass on its own. Next, Howe's pedal steel swaps solos with his own electric guitar. It is always a challenge to play this live, but Howe seems to be able to manage it, even in his 70s. Mellotron dominates the 'Hold Down The Window' section, an atmospheric interlude until we are back into the main theme again briefly, followed by the wonderfully tense and atmospheric 'outboard river' section, essentially a hugely evocative, yet also meaningless word list, with some inspired rhymes. This is clearly Anderson combining words for their sound rather than their meaning, but it works brilliantly. The section builds, with Mellotron and acoustic guitar dominant, soon joined by bass and Bruford's agile snare. With the tension broken, we are back into the main riff again and, after a final wordless vocal interlude, the track finishes on a terrific solo from Howe.

Another winning live track, 'Siberian Khatru' has most often been used as an opening piece – most notably on the *Close To The Edge* tour, the *Tormato* tour and the *Tales* tour. When not being used as an opener, it is usually not played at all.

Although I am not a huge fan of Yes cover versions, I do love the Stanley Snail version on *Tales From Yesterday* – a Yes tribute album from 1996, which delivers a very faithful version of the track but wittily replaces the harpsichord solo with a section of 'The Sahara Of Snow Part One' from the Bruford album *One Of A Kind* – a personal favourite.

Above: Yes rehearsing around 1971-1972.

Yes Live In 1972 And 1973

Yessongs

Personnel:
Jon Anderson: vocals
Chris Squire: bass, vocals
Steve Howe: guitars, vocals
Alan White: drums
Rick Wakeman: keyboards
Bill Bruford: Drums on 'Perpetual Change', 'Long Distance Runaround' and 'The Fish'
Produced by Yes and Eddie Offord
Mixed at Advision Studios
Co-ordination: Brian Lane
Recording engineer: Geoff Haslam
Released: May 1973
Highest chart places: UK: 7, US: 12
Running time: 129:16
Tracklist:
1. 'Opening (Excerpt From 'Firebird Suite')', 2. 'Siberian Khatru', 3. 'Heart Of The Sunrise', 4. 'Perpetual Change', 5. 'And You And I', 6. 'Mood For A Day', 7. 'Excerpts From The Six Wives Of Henry VIII', 8. 'Roundabout', 9. 'I've Seen All Good People', 10. 'Long Distance Runaround/The Fish', 11. 'Close To The Edge', 12. 'Yours Is No Disgrace', 13. 'Starship Trooper'

While triple albums were not exactly unheard of in 1973 – George Harrison's *All Things Must Pass* had been released in 1970, for instance – Yes were the first 1970s band to present their live recordings in such a comprehensive format. The six sides of vinyl total over two hours, the point being to reproduce a Yes show as an audience might experience it, with solo spots in place.

Many shows were recorded during 1972, initially with Bill Bruford as the band continued to promote *Fragile*, and as a result, he appears on 'Perpetual Change' and 'Long Distance Runaround/The Fish', both of which were initially dropped as the band played shorter sets in 1972 than would be customary by 1974, especially as they often had an opening act, especially when playing in the US.

It's also notable that no tracks from before *The Yes Album* are featured. There was a certain feeling at the time that the Yes of the first two albums was something of a different band, especially as Banks and Kaye were no longer present, and so the entire triple is made up of songs from *The Yes Album*, *Fragile* and *Close To The Edge*. This attitude was not always to be the case. Time provides perspective, and by the mid-1970s, the occasional song from that era had made its way into the set, with the band paying tribute to their earliest incarnation right up to the present day.

There are a few omissions, of course. That 'Clap' doesn't appear might be considered a surprise considering its ubiquity in later years, but its album version is a live performance anyway. 'A Venture' was never well favoured, and 'South Side Of The Sky' was attempted live, but, surprisingly, the band didn't think it worked as already discussed. It was to have its time of glory in much later years.

Only 'The Fish' and 'Mood For A Day' of the solo pieces from *Fragile* are included, although Wakeman's spectacular solo set was (mainly) from *The Six Wives Of Henry VIII,* which, let us not forget, had not been released at that point.

Much has been made of the album's sound quality, which is sometimes harsh, murky and echoey, and of Squire's bass being mixed somewhat low, which doesn't make for easy listening, especially on substandard audio equipment. It does have a suitably 'in the room' vibe to it, though. For the Yes fan, the choice is either to struggle with the poor sound and relatively primitive instrumentation (there are no acoustic textures in the full-band pieces aside from some piano due to the extreme technical limitations) despite the top-notch sound system the band were using, or to look beyond those considerations and hear the performances.

There's no doubt that this version of the band, especially with the high-energy Alan White behind the kit, was on fire. Despite exactly the same personnel, this was not the road-honed behemoth that existed by 1979, with all its texture and subtlety. This was a youthful rock band playing complex material lightning fast, with huge energy and skill. It's also clear that in 1972 they had no fear. Listen to Steve Howe's improvisation in 'Perpetual Change' and 'Yours Is No Disgrace'. He's trying things and failing sometimes, but it doesn't matter. The thrill is in the attempt. Yes would never play with this level of on-the-edge-of-your-seat risk-taking again.

However, some of this was probably more exciting to experience live than it is on the album. Some of the live versions – 'Roundabout' and 'Starship Trooper' being obvious examples – have been superseded by better versions more recently. However, *Yessongs* set the template for how Yes would approach live performance for the next 50 years.

Yessongs The Movie

Recorded on 16 December 1972 at The Rainbow Theatre, London
Recorded and mixed by Eddie Offord, assisted by Mike Dunn
Lighting: Mike Tait
Directed by Peter Neal
Edited by Philip Howe
Produced by David Speechley
Executive producer: Brian Lane
Released: 1975
Tracklist:

1. 'Opening (Excerpt From 'Close To The Edge')' 2. 'I've Seen All Good People' 3. 'Clap' 4. 'And You And I' 4. 'Close To The Edge' 5. 'Rick Wakeman Solo (Incorporating Excerpts From Six Wives Of Henry VIII, 'Jingle Bells' And 'The Hallelujah Chorus')', 6. 'Roundabout' 7. 'Yours Is No Disgrace'
Yessongs 40 Years On Blu-ray extras:
Steve Howe: Beginnings
Films of three tracks from Howe's 1975 solo album
2012 documentary featuring Chris Squire, Steve Howe and Roger Dean

The film, recorded towards the end of the *Close To The Edge* tour, offers a fascinating insight into how rock bands appeared on stage in the early 1970s. At that point, a filmed live performance outside a TV studio was a rarity, and this movie came about because Howe's brother, Philip, was a film editor.

First of all, it's not the whole set played that night, since 'Siberian Khatru', 'Mood For A Day', 'Heart Of The Sunrise' and 'Starship Trooper' were also played and are much missed, and the audio, while decent, has the same 'back of the auditorium' feel that *Yessongs* has. However, the performances are great, and (perhaps by coincidence) the camera spends a lot of time on Howe's face. There's no additional lighting, so the movie feels quite dark, although not unbearably so. Other points of note:

On stage, Anderson is not the ultra-confident figure he would become by the later 1970s. He was still learning his stagecraft at that point. He sings well, however.

By contrast to Howe, Wakeman is lost in a mane of long blond hair, but plays astonishingly well bedecked in his sequin-encrusted cape, accentuated by a mirror behind him. His solo, which includes 'Jingle Bells' played as a blues, is typically playful. Note also, however, the taped church organ part dropped in by Eddie Offord during *Close To The Edge*.

After a barnstorming 'And You And I', the editor cuts to the seated audience. Few of the front row are applauding, and someone also appears to be asleep.

The 2012 40th anniversary Blu-ray includes a short film by Steve Howe, performing 'Ram', 'Beginnings' with Patrick Moraz on harpsichord and 'Break Away From It All' complete with bucolic visuals. An overlong documentary features talking-head interviews with Howe, Squire and Roger Dean. It's fine but reveals very little that fans won't already know or have guessed.

Although parts of the movie were shown on *The Old Grey Whistle Test* as early as 1973, it didn't get a limited cinema release in the US until 1975. By this time, Wakeman had left the band and was a considerable name, so his name appears slightly larger and at the top of personnel listings on promotional posters.

Progeny: Seven Shows From Seventy Two and Progeny: Highlights From Seventy Two

Recorded in North America between 31 October and 20 November 1972
Production, mixing: Brian Kehew

Production: Steve Woolard, Carmine Rubino, Geoff Haslam, Mike Dunn
Released in May 2015 on Rhino Records
Highest chart placings: none
Tracklist:
Disc One: 1. 'Opening (Excerpt from Firebird Suite) by Igor Stravinsky, 2.Siberian Khatru' 3. 'I've Seen All Good People', 4. 'Mood For A Day/Clap', 5. 'Heart Of The Sunrise', 6. 'And You And I'
Disc Two: 1. 'Close To The Edge', 2. 'Excerpts From The Six Wives Of Henry VIII', 3.'Roundabout', 4. 'Yours Is No Disgrace'

While some of the material for *Yessongs* was compiled from shows in the UK, not least the shows at The Rainbow in December 1972 that were used for the *Yessongs* movie, some of it was taken from a batch of shows recorded in the US a few weeks earlier.

Recordings from seven of these shows were unearthed and an attempt was made to mix them by well-known producer and technician Brian Kehew. This attempt was not initially successful, since the audio files were no better than those used to create *Yessongs*. However, they soon realised that the Dolby on the tape machines had been incorrectly calibrated, so the team set about adjusting every instrument by ear.

The result, sonically, is a distinct improvement on the audio of *Yessongs,* and presents, for those interested enough, the same set played seven times over the course of 19 days. The differences are fairly subtle, and so very much for those, especially bootleg lovers, who love to track a tour and get a feel for the nuances of live performance.

The highlights double CD will be enough for four out of five listeners, including your author, but it's still an essential purchase, and all seven shows are available on streaming services.

Tales From Topographic Oceans (1973)

Personnel:
Jon Anderson: vocals, guitar, percussion
Chris Squire: bass, vocals
Steve Howe: guitars, vocals
Alan White: drums, percussion, piano
Rick Wakeman: keyboards
Produced at Morgan Studios, London, by Yes and Eddie Offord, July- September 1973
Engineer: Nigel Luby
Co-ordination: Brian Lane
Released: December 1973
Highest chart places: UK: 1, US: 6
Running time: 81:15

Most albums in the Yes catalogue spark debate among fans. Sometimes, as with *Close To The Edge,* the debate is simply about whether it is the greatest album they ever made, or whether it is simply in the top three. In other cases, like *Open Your Eyes* from 1997, for instance, the conversation tends to revolve around how poor it is. No album, however, has as much debate about its status within the band's discography as *Tales From Topographic Oceans*. For some – many, in fact – it is the crowning achievement of the band. For some, it is even the pinnacle of the progressive rock era. Yet for others, probably closer to a broader consensus, it is hugely flawed. To those listeners, it contains some strong material, but spread too thinly, a prisoner of the album's overriding mission to present four tracks over four sides of a record for the first time. So, is it a bold masterpiece or a white elephant?

Let us first remember how far the band had come in little over four years. To date, each album had shown a huge leap in confidence, not to mention playing and compositional skill. Both Steve Howe and Rick Wakeman had added huge amounts to the band. Howe provided versatility and a daring sense of experimentation, while Wakeman added dexterity, a taste for technology and the ability to stitch pieces of music together so that they worked as a whole. But the five musicians also worked as an (albeit dysfunctional) unit. The arrival of Alan White, with his ferocious drumming and laid-back personality, possibly took a little of the band's combativeness out, creatively.

Additionally, *Close To The Edge* had been created very much by the band as a single, rather tortuous unit, but it was Anderson and Howe who provided the lyrical and musical backbone that led to the creation of *Tales*. With two members taking the lead, the other three needed to be 'sold' the concept. It was not to be an easy task.

The two had conceived the album on tour during the spring of 1973 when Anderson read about the four Shastras in a footnote to the *Autobiography Of*

A Yogi by Paramahansa Yogananda, which had been given to him by Jamie Muir of King Crimson. In translating this into four long-form pieces, Anderson was also aspiring to symphonic works in the fashion of Sibelius or Mahler, a process begun on *Close To The Edge*.

This approach should be seen in the context of a natural, if ambitious, progression from that album. He and Steve Howe put together the lyrical and thematic basis of the album during that tour, finalising their ideas later that spring before beginning recording during the summer and autumn of 1973.

Anderson still had some strange ideas along the way. He wanted to record using a mobile studio in the countryside, which led the crew to put bales of hay and cut-out cows in Morgan Studios. He also asked for a tiled vocal booth to give him the sort of sound he got from singing in his bathroom. It didn't work. But by this time, the rest of the band had, somewhat reluctantly, agreed to Anderson and Howe's structure. Squire and Alan White, who was making his first appearance on a Yes studio album, let us not forget, bought into the project, making considerable contributions to the album. However, Wakeman was not enamoured of the material, and even though, as the Steven Wilson remix reveals, he is present throughout the album, his contributions are muted.

Even on 'The Revealing Science Of God', which includes his thrilling Minimoog solo towards the climax of the piece, some of his playing feels superficial. His sound palette, too, seems unimaginative. While there is some Hammond and piano dotted around, he mainly sticks to Minimoog and Mellotron, often playing them together. Admittedly, these two instruments work very well together, but by contrast, Howe's palette is constantly – even thrillingly – inventive. In short, Wakeman is present, but he doesn't really contribute much creatively.

Tales is an elusive, frustrating album in many ways. Of course, going in with four 20-minute pieces in mind from the start was arguably foolhardy and compared to the band at its most concise, almost every piece seems overextended, with sections regularly repeated. On the other hand, good ideas aren't developed enough, especially during 'The Remembering'. And yet, *Tales* remains my most-played Yes album. It has a tone unlike any other recording in the catalogue. I think the reason I enjoy it so much is that, unlike the slice of near-perfection that is *Close To The Edge*, its flaws are laid bare and very human. This time you could hear the band struggling a little, in a sense, trying to mould their ideas into four neat, 20-minute parcels but still producing something of sweeping invention in the end.

What *Tales* does not deserve is the derision it has been subjected to for at least 20 years, not least from its keyboard player. It became one of the symbols, not just of the pomposity of progressive rock, but of the silliness of it. For many years, the two-word phrase 'prog rock' became one of derision, of a movement that should never have happened. Oh, how we fans suffered in those years!

But on the whole, *Tales* was considered a disappointment, even with friends of the band, like journalist Chris Welch, who generally thought that the band had gone too far in their ambition with this one, saying in *Melody Maker* at the time:

> It is a fragmented masterpiece, assembled with loving care and long hours in the studio. Brilliant in patches, but often taking far too long to make its various points, and curiously lacking in warmth or personal expression.

Later in the decade, it was held up as an example of the excesses of the 'old guard' – the sort of bloated, excessive music that needed to be swept away. It's not hard to see why. The band exacerbated this by playing the album in its entirety on tour in the UK before it had been released. Indeed, it was only in the spring of 1974 that they began to drop 'The Remembering' from the set. For Wakeman, the tour was to be his last work with Yes for two and a half years.

There's a fascinating interview with Howe and Wakeman, filmed in New York in February 1974 on the *Tales* tour with Bob Harris for *The Old Grey Whistle Test*. Wakeman looks bloated and tired, and while he talks a fair amount, there's little of his trademark humour. He only animates when discussing receiving the cut (the initial vinyl test pressing) of his album *Journey To The Centre Of The Earth*, which had been recorded live just three weeks before the US tour. Howe is very careful to tell Harris that there would be a Yes album, which seems to surprise Wakeman. Three months later, he'd left the band just as *Journey* reached number one in the UK album charts.

'The Revealing Science Of God (Dance Of The Dawn)' (Anderson, Howe, Squire, Wakeman, White)

Of the four 'movements' on *Tales*, 'The Revealing Science Of God' and 'Ritual' are the band's most revived pieces over the years, the former being played at the *Keys To Ascension* shows in 1996 and also on the *Open Your Eyes* tour in 1998, plus the *Tales* tours in 2017 and 2018. There are many Yes tribute bands worldwide, and 'The Revealing Science Of God' is usually the piece from *Tales* they attempt first. Accessible and well-structured, it is the track that gets the balance between instrumentation just about right, with some superb contributions from Wakeman, particularly some terrific piano in the up-tempo 'Starlight, movement...' section, and of course, his astonishing Minimoog solo towards the end of the piece, surely his most thrilling contribution to any Yes studio album.

Yet in the 'perfect edit in my head', I think I would still lose three or four minutes. The track has a superb beginning – Anderson's chanted vocals and the gradual build of instruments leading into the opening Minimoog theme is exquisite. Some later versions of the track – most notably the Rhino remaster – have an ambient opening that was dropped for the final mix on the original version. This addition, in my view, lessens the impact of the chanted beginning and was quite rightly removed for the 1973 double-album set.

The track soon settles into a bit of a mid-tempo plod, however, with Howe soloing rather aimlessly, although the 'chorus' such as it is, is masterful, even catchy. Things improve during the powerful 'starlight, movement...' section, but this idea is dispensed with very quickly, replaced by another rather aimless section, although the 'rape the forest' vocal part with its dramatic Minimoog is excellent, followed by a return to the up-tempo section, and a terrifically inventive solo section from Howe.

The 'young Christians' section – revived from the attempt to create a song from it in 1971 – is also wonderful, but the instrumental section that follows it takes rather too long to make its point, and Wakeman's solo, as we all know, is thrilling, made twice as good by the brilliance of the ensemble playing behind it and all the better for its brevity.

The track finishes with a restatement of the main theme – the sort of classically-inspired technique that the band were becoming masters of.

Despite my reservations, 'The Revealing Science Of God' is a terrific start, made all the better by the fact that both Howe and Wakeman seem fully engaged and playing in harmony. Would it continue?

'The Remembering (High The Memory)' (Anderson, Howe, Squire, Wakeman, White)

The first of the two supposedly problematic movements, 'The Remembering' is an odd, low-key piece of music. In many ways, it is lovely. It is tuneful and well played, particularly by Chris Squire, whose bass playing is a delicate delight throughout the track. The problem is that it doesn't really go anywhere; the arrangement is too linear, drifting along for a good nine minutes, with little Mellotron and Moog passages that seem to lack imagination in themselves. Only when the 'force between the mouth of freedom' section kicks in, with some acoustic textures at last, does the piece leap into life. The following 'Relayer' section is terrific, classic Yes at their best, with Wakeman's Moog to the fore, but it is over for the first time frustratingly quickly. The whole pattern repeats, ending again in trite atmospherics. The piece ends well with a brief surge of excitement before petering out again. It is unclear whether Wakeman was not engaged enough to come up with something better here, or whether the piece's requirements did not suit his style. Probably both are true.

It is no wonder this side was a challenging live proposition for both the band and the audience. The frustrating thing is that this track has so much promise, some great melodies and some superb playing, as you might expect, but having played it dozens of times over 50 years, I still find it an infuriating listening experience. It is a structural problem, I think, falling into repetition far too easily. Somewhere in there, there is a superb ten-minute piece trying to get out. 'The Remembering' was played on the *Tales* tour, although it was dropped in the second European leg in the early spring of 1974.

It was finally revived in a very short (about three-minute) section when the band played a cleverly arranged *Tales* medley on tour during 2024.

I do understand the reverence some listeners have for it. This is a different Yes following a more ambient path, and for some this is just what they wanted from the band. But it's a bit of a sonic *cul-de-sac* for Yes, perhaps hampered by its structure, which makes it very difficult to play live in its entirety as part of a rock show. But for many, it's the epitome of what makes this most immersive of albums the great work of art that it is. Music is, after all, supremely subjective, and one man's frustration is another man's nirvana. Playing the piece again in 2023, I am struck by how magnificent the 'Relayer' section is. That it lies buried in a piece of music that is probably considered unplayable as a whole is somewhat annoying.

'The Ancient (Giants Under The Sun)' (Anderson, Howe, Squire, Wakeman, White)

Despite its difficult reputation, I like 'The Ancient'. I appreciate that little suggestion of jazz, the precursor of *Relayer,* and I admire the atmosphere that it creates. This is not just fashioned from the textures of Steve Howe's guitars, but from the invention in Alan White's percussion arrangements.

Unlike 'The Remembering', there is real structure here. The opening instrumental section sets things up before the Mellotron-led opening vocal passage and the tense instrumental section that follows it. So far, so good, and very Yes. In fact, there is nothing in the first eight minutes or so that is out of keeping with anything the band had produced on *Tales* or before. The 'trouble', if indeed trouble it is, comes roughly between the nine and 12-minute marks, when the track veers off into free jazz, Frank Zappa territory. If this were King Crimson, this section would be hailed for the invention of Fripp's guitar work, but in Yes? Well, why not?

In context, this is barely three minutes before the piece resolves itself into the acoustic introduction of the famous 'Leaves Of Green' section, with one of Steve Howe's best-loved classical guitar pieces and a charming, delicate vocal from Anderson. It seems to me that three minutes of rather 'wild' music in the middle of an otherwise challenging but relatively accessible piece has turned many listeners, and possibly a certain keyboard player, away from a track that they would otherwise find very rewarding.

'The Ancient' was played live on the 1974 *Tales* tour but has not been played since. However, the 'Leaves Of Green' section has appeared fairly regularly on setlists whenever Howe has been in the band. It was occasionally played, for instance, on the *Tormato* tour in 1978-1979 and on the 2017-2018 *Topographic* tours, as well as the 2024 *Classic Tales* tour.

'Ritual (Nous Sommes Du Soleil)' (Anderson, Howe, Squire, Wakeman, White)

Always the masters of the big finish, 'Ritual' sees the band concluding the album in some style, although, as with the rest of the album, not every moment is successful. What 'Ritual' does have, however, is proper coherence throughout its 22 minutes. The piece begins in fine style, with Squire's thumping bass vying for space with Howe's guitar, and some nice, understated synthesizer from Wakeman. Indeed, the Wilson remix reveals more of this, previously lost in the mix. The bass solo is short, and Howe's reprise of some of his own guitar themes from earlier in the album works nicely. The main theme – 'Nous Somme Du Soleil' (we are of the sun) is beautiful. It's one of Anderson's prettiest tunes, with a sort of Gallic 'torch song' feel crossed with some strong harmonies in the Crosby, Stills & Nash style, largely accompanied by Howe's electric sitar, much used on this album.

The 'open doors' vocals section overstays its welcome just a touch but does at least build nicely into the bass/percussion section.

If the track has a problem, it is mainly in the second part of this instrumental section, which features White's percussion, played against his own drum solo, which genuinely feels like it belongs on a live album. Much extended in the band's live performances, there is some visual spectacle here, but on the album it feels like filler, well-played and mixed though it is. Anderson's reprise of the main theme is touching, and the slow build of the track's climax is powerful and yet understated.

Like the 'Revealing Science Of God', 'Ritual' has made numerous appearances in the live set, but until the *Topographic* tour of 2017/18, the tracks had never appeared together in the same set since the initial *Tales* tour. It was the only piece to make it into the Moraz era and was played on the *Relayer* tour. It was also played on the 2000 *Masterworks* tour in the US and on the 2004 *World* tour, as well as part of the aforementioned 2024 *Classic Tales* tour.

Relayer (1974)

Personnel:
Jon Anderson: vocals
Steve Howe: electric and acoustic guitars, pedal steel, vocals
Chris Squire: bass, vocals
Alan White: drums, percussion
Patrick Moraz: keyboards
Produced at New Pipers, Virginia Water, on the Rolling Stones Mobile by Yes and Eddie Offord, Summer 1974
Tape operator: Gennaro Rippo.
Co-ordination: Brian Lane.
UK release date: November 1974
US release date: December 1974
Highest chart places: UK: 4, US: 5
Running time: 40:31

Rick Wakeman left Yes in May 1974 within a few weeks of the final dates on the *Tales* tour, having disliked that album and much of the tour that went with it. He had also had huge success with his second solo album, *Journey To The Centre Of The Earth*. Feeling unable to contribute to the new music the band were developing, he decided to move on.

This gave the band a problem. They couldn't just bring in another Tony Kaye; they needed someone with a technique as well developed as Rick's, not to mention similar technological skills. The band spent several weeks over the course of the early summer auditioning keyboard players, the highest profile of these being Vangelis, the enigmatic Greek musician. There's an interesting alternative reality where Vangelis is offered and accepts the job. But the musician would have to have toned down his individualistic tendencies to work within such a supposedly democratic band, not to mention the need to become accustomed to travel as a touring musician. Vangelis hated to fly. With the Greek's keyboards still in the studio, a converted garage at New Pipers – Chris Squire's house in Virginia Water in Surrey – Swiss musician Patrick Moraz tried out, and jaws dropped.

Moraz had previously been in a Swiss band called Mainhorse and had then, effectively, replaced Keith Emerson in The Nice, with the band renaming themselves Refugee. A versatile, fluid and flamboyant player, the striking Moraz, with his classical good looks, cleft chin and shock of dark hair, had some of Wakeman's showmanship but also a strong interest in jazz fusion. This new form of music, which blended the harmonic complexity of jazz with the speed and power of rock, developed in parallel with progressive rock in the late 1960s and early 1970s via Miles Davis and later supergroups like The Mahavishnu Orchestra and Return To Forever. Despite neither musician's style being ideally suited to jazz, Squire and White, in particular, were beginning to draw on such influences in the new music they were writing.

Moraz seemed a perfect fit.

Recording began immediately at New Pipers using the Rolling Stones Mobile and continued through the summer and early autumn with Eddie Offord again at the helm for the last time. The band retrenched to the *Close To The Edge* format, with one long side of music and two mid-length pieces, and taken as a whole, *Relayer* is a bold, brash and very rewarding piece of work. However, it is not for the faint-hearted. In 'Gates Of Delirium', the band produced the most atonal and difficult work of their career. It is beloved of many, hated by a minority. 'Sound Chaser' is pure indulgence, a glorious melting pot of mad ideas, while 'To Be Over' has Anderson returning to his theme of 'the river', a truly languid and beautiful piece of music. Overall, the album has a unique tone in the Yes catalogue. It is the only recording to have a marked jazz influence outside the odd moment elsewhere (the scatting on 'Roundabout' being one, of course), but also one which embraces influences – again mainly from Anderson and Howe – in the more atonal classical works of composers like Stravinsky and Shostakovich.

There is a brightness to the sound on the album, which comes not just from the lightness of Moraz's keyboard textures, but also directly from Howe's main choice of guitar, the Fender Broadcaster, an instrument better known for use in country music, with its fragile, treble-oriented sound. The results are extraordinary.

Once again, the album was understandably given a mixed reception, although it performed well commercially. Played in its entirety during 1974 and 1975, 'To Be Over' was dropped for the *Solo Albums* tour in 1976, and with Wakeman returning to the band for 1977 dates, the album was understandably dropped entirely except for the 'Soon' section of 'The Gates Of Delirium', played in 'The Big Medley' in 1978 and 1979. The other two tracks have never been played since by the whole band, so associated with Patrick Moraz are they, although Steve Howe plays an excellent solo guitar version of 'To Be Over'. 'The Gates Of Delirium' has been played on a few tours since – on the *Masterworks* tour in 2000 and the *Symphonic* tour a year later, then finally on the *Royal Affair* tour in 2019.

Frustratingly, from a fan's point of view, a proposed *Relayer* tour in 2020, postponed to 2022 and then cancelled completely, was planned but seems once again to be highly unlikely. Jon Anderson also played 'Gates' at shows in 2023 with The Band Geeks.

'The Gates Of Delirium' (Anderson, Howe, Squire, White, Moraz)

At just under 22 intense minutes, 'The Gates Of Delirium' remains the longest individual studio piece in the Yes discography. At a time in the 21st century when long tracks in progressive rock are commonplace, this can often point towards mindless tedium or that the piece is a series of 'bits' strung together (see 'That, That Is' in the next volume). Not so with this astonishing piece of music. Even more than 'Close To The Edge', this is a track that demands to be the length it is. It would be impossible to class any of this 'song' as 'filler' – it is far too intense a ride for that.

'Gates' was brought to the band by Anderson in rudimentary form, and played badly on piano – including the 'battle' section. Based very, very loosely on *War And Peace* by Tolstoy, the lyrics are Anderson's best on any Yes album, beautifully straddling genuine meaning with his usual obliqueness.

The short (two-minute) instrumental introduction is interesting for several reasons. It heralds some themes that we will hear later in the piece; it gives us a glimpse of the form (fearsome) and tone (bright) that Howe will be bringing to the table, and finally, it introduces us to Patrick Moraz and this early version of 'soundscaping'. On this track, in particular, his tone and palette are more important than his ability to solo. Having become used to Wakeman's arsenal of instruments, we now get Moraz's. It is very fresh, to the extent that sometimes we don't quite know what instrument is making a particular sound. It's exciting and unsettling, too. It's perfectly fine to wish he'd made more Yes music.

The first vocal section ('Stand and fight we do consider...') is relatively low-key but builds as the acoustic instruments (mandolin or similar) are gradually abandoned, and we hear Moraz solo on synthesizer for the first time. By the five-minute mark, we are in the midst of a more intense, almost hard-rocking section. The 'Listen should we fight forever...' section introduces the doubt that everyone feels in war until 'kill or be killed' becomes the more vital emotion. Again, the music builds with Howe playing the main melodic theme, and then at eight minutes, 'The fist will run...' unleashes hell...

We now have to wait ten minutes before the next vocal passage, yet the track continues twisting and turning, initially with Howe and Moraz taking it in turns to play the melody, with an intense, jazzy rhythm section. At 10:25, however, the piece shifts into another gear, dominated by Squire's thunderous, fusion bass, and we start to hear percussive crashes, as the battle itself gets underway, and Howe's soloing becomes more atonal. The 'war' noises become more powerful, Squire and White keep up a thunderous level of intensity, and then the track threatens to implode, regaining its structure at 12.50 with a superb synthesizer melody line from Moraz – complete with his favourite tool – plenty of pitch bend – until Howe takes up the same theme, switching, via a final bass run from Squire, to pedal steel and it's time for 'Soon'.

Many who find the first 16 minutes of 'Gates Of Delirium' unpalatable make an exception for this beautiful, uplifting final section. It features some delicate pedal steel from Howe and a wonderfully fragile vocal from Anderson, but Moraz's keyboards should not be underestimated either, initially played on organ, then Mellotron. It is a beautiful piece, and yet it still feels connected to the whole. A single version of 'Soon' was, understandably, released, and the band have played this segment of the song live more often than the full piece from which it comes.

'Sound Chaser' (Anderson, Howe, Squire, White, Moraz)
'From the sublime to the ridiculous' may be a cliché, but here it really is appropriate. 'Sound Chaser' is, in itself, delirious. It is structured like a bad dream – just as you feel you are settling into the track, it takes you somewhere else. It begins with Moraz's Fender Rhodes (and just a touch of Mellotron) and White's percussion – beginning with cymbals, then a drum solo of sorts – dominating. We then hurtle into a lightning-fast, jazzy section, with Howe and Squire playing the same line, then the first vocal section – with Howe, White and Squire playing at full speed – while Moraz and Anderson deal with the actual melody. Squire and Howe keep up the pace before the track breaks down into a hugely indulgent, partially-unaccompanied electric flamenco solo (this is the territory of famed fusion guitarist Al Di Meola) followed by a slower section, again dominated by Howe and White's timpani. A moment of stillness, a quiet vocal passage from Anderson, then a reprise of the opening, but this time followed by an almost lopsided, swinging section dominated by pedal steel and Mellotron, fast then slow. But wait – then we have Anderson singing 'cha, cha, cha', a fluid and lengthy Moog solo, underpinned by some astonishing bass from Squire, a final fast section which seems to feature every theme in the song at the same time, one more set of 'cha, cha's' and we're out...

What should we make of 'Sound Chaser'? It's magnificent in many ways, yet it probably represents progressive rock at its most indulgent. While it is Howe and Moraz that get to play the 'flashy' bits, the real stars are White and Squire. White is allowed to hit many, many different pieces of percussion, loud and quiet, while Squire – who played with a pick, let us not forget – produces some runs so fast that one almost wonders if they were sped up in the studio.

Only in the years 1974 or 1975 could a track like this have been created – and released – and still get into the top ten of the album charts on both sides of the Atlantic. Oh, and it opened the set for almost two years of touring, as well. It is mind-altering, bonkers stuff.

'To Be Over' (Anderson, Howe, Squire, White, Moraz)
Back to the sublime again with this glorious, sometimes unsung classic. I say unsung because it can sometimes be overlooked after the bluster and flash of the two previous tracks. However, this is a place of serenity, a piece of music that really 'flows downstream', led initially by Howe's electric sitar and Moraz's synthesizer, but dominated by Howe's pedal steel and Fender Broadcaster combo, as the rest of the album has been. Yes always know how to end an album, and the gentle build towards the final vocal section and Moraz's lovely Moog solo feel like a prelude to the climax of 'Awaken' three years later, but here the piece fades to nothing. It is a poised and supremely controlled masterpiece.

The band looking unusually relaxed in Regent's Park, London, during a photoshoot for the *Tormato* album cover in 1978. (*Jim Halley*)

Left: Yes in 1968. L to R: Peter Banks, Chris Squire, Tony Kaye, Jon Anderson and Tony O'Reilly, who was the short-lived replacement for Bill Bruford for a few weeks.

Right: *Yes*. The somewhat dated UK cover of the debut album, featuring the 'speech bubble' logo. (*Atlantic*)

Left: The US cover of the debut, with a full band photo taken in London. (*Atlantic*)

Right: 'Looking Around', the band's early single, released in 1969. (*Atlantic*)

Left: *Time And A Word*. The bold UK cover was designed by Laurence Sackman. (*Atlantic*)

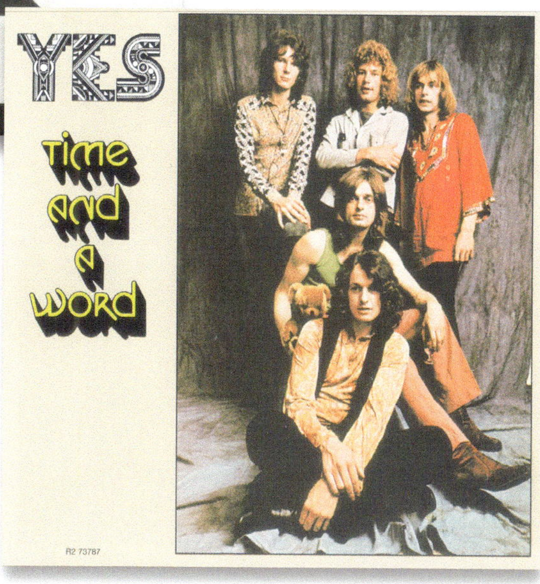

Right: Atlantic took no chances with the US cover, however, and with Banks out of the band, Steve Howe is featured. (*Atlantic*)

Left: Peter Banks – the first lineup change of many.

Right: A lanky Chris Squire in 1969. Nice hat. (*Capitol/ Universal Music*)

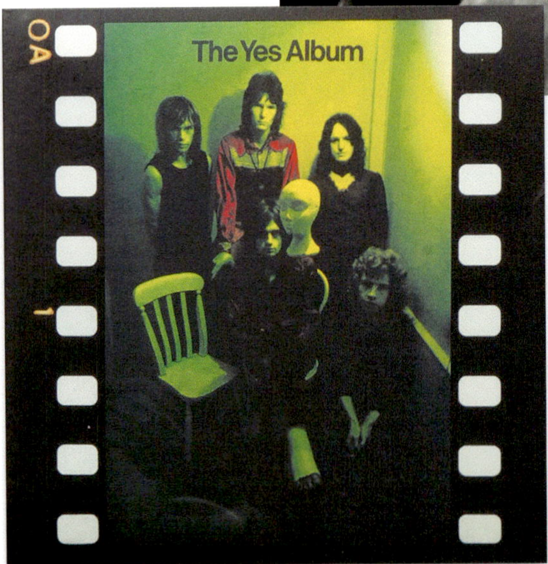

Left: *The Yes Album*. This was the band's breakthrough album in the UK. Note the plaster of Kaye's ankle, the result of a road accident on the way back from a gig in Basingstoke. (*Atlantic*)

Right: A psychedelic Howe plays 'Yours Is No Disgrace' on German TV in 1971.

Left: Jon Anderson, who was already a performing veteran in his mid-20s, having been a member of Lancashire band The Warriors.

Right: A youthful Bill 'Tubs' Bruford, on British TV during the *Fragile* era.

Left: Roger Dean's Yes debut was the remarkable cover for *Fragile,* which also marked the debut of Rick Wakeman. The spacecraft became Dean's 'signature'. (*Atlantic*)

Right: A 21-year-old Rick Wakeman photographed in 1971, with Hammond, Mellotron and several cans of Long Life light ale.

Left: The remarkable but increasingly eccentric Eddie Offord, who engineered every album up to *Relayer* except the debut and was the band's live sound engineer until 1976.

Right: Dean followed *Fragile* with the bold cover for *Close To The Edge*. The classic Yes logo debuted. (*Atlantic*)

Below: Dean's fantastical landscape that graced the inner gatefold of *Close To The Edge*. (*Atlantic*)

Right: The cover of *Tales From Topographic Oceans* is, if anything, even more distinctive. It's a remarkable window into the tone of this flawed album. (*Atlantic*)

Left: Dean's cover for the triple live album *Yessongs*. The paintings inside are wonderful, even if the front cover is somewhat dated. (*Atlantic*)

Right: Dean's cover for *Progeny: Highlights From Seventy-Two*. The highlights package from a six-album set, presenting remixed and recalibrated live shows from the US on the *Close To The Edge* tour. (*Rhino*)

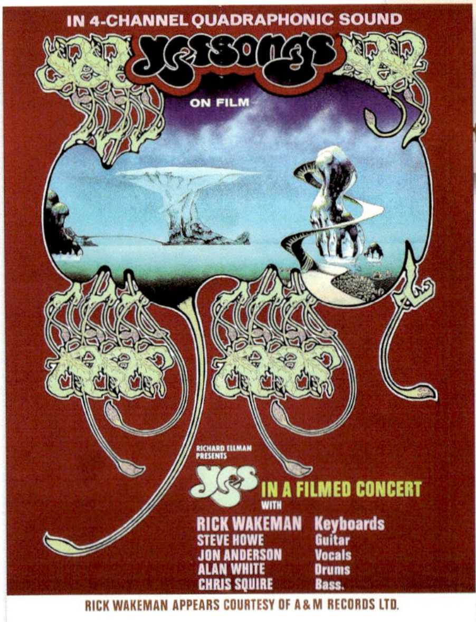

Left: *Yessongs* the movie wasn't released theatrically until 1975, by which time Rick Wakeman was a bestselling solo artist, thus the larger font for his name on the poster.

Right: The fourth Dean cover was for *Relayer,* Patrick Moraz's only Yes album with the band. (*Atlantic*)

Left: Patrick Moraz and a Micro Moog show off some Yes merchandise circa 1976.

Right: *Live At Roosevelt Stadium 1976.* An official 2026 release for this Moraz-era show from the summer of 1976. (*Rhino*)

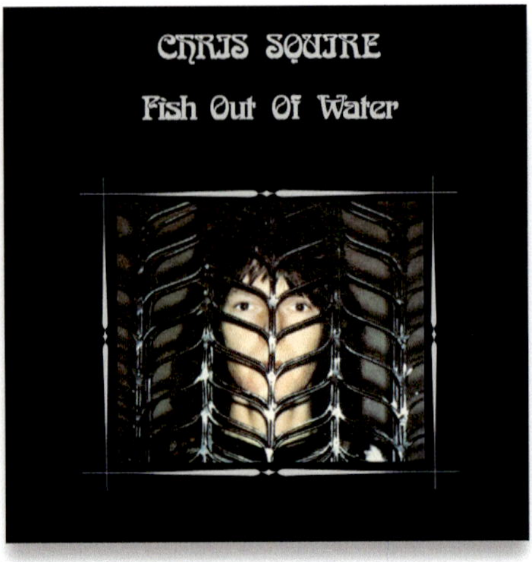

This page: Released during 1975 and 1976, the five solo albums from the period couldn't be more different. (*Atlantic*)

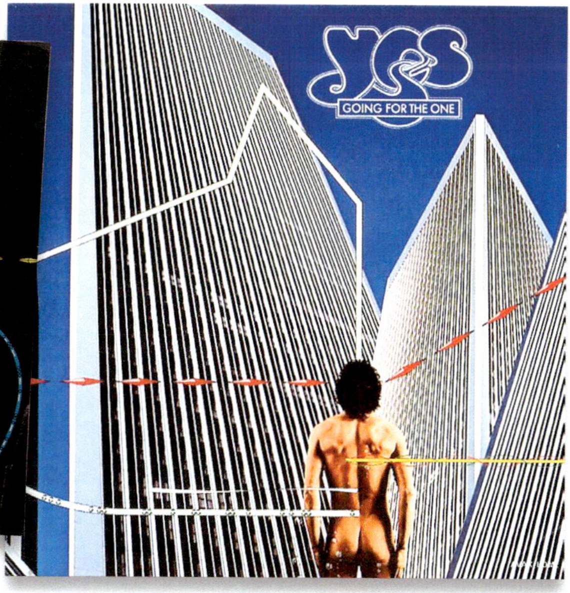

Above right: It was all change for *Going For The One*, with the ultra-trendy Hipgnosis handling the cover design and Wakeman back in the band. (*Atlantic*)
Above left: The programme from the *Yesshows* tour of 1977. (*Bruce Strickland*)
Below left: The harmony was short-lived. *Tormato* found the band struggling with arrangements and the group's overall direction. (*Atlantic*)
Below right: ...even if it did spawn a lengthy and hugely successful world tour with the band playing in the round. (*Stephen Lambe*)

Left: *Drama*. 1980. After some aborted sessions in Paris, the band fragmented, with Anderson and Wakeman replaced by Trevor Horn and Geoff Downes. It was to be quite a year! (*Atlantic*)

Right: A publicity shot of the *Drama*-era band. (*Atlantic*)

Left: *Yesshows*. A decent, if flawed, second live album, mixed by Chris Squire and released without the consent of most of the band. (*Atlantic*)

Right: Still a year away from becoming Yes, Cinema relax during rehearsals in London during the summer of 1982. (*David Watkinson Collection*)

Left: Tony Kaye rehearsing with Cinema. (*David Watkinson Collection*)

Right: Trevor Rabin and Alan White in full flight with Cinema at the John Henry practice studio in London. (*David Watkinson Collection*)

Left: Yes make a triumphant return with the ultra-modern *90125* at the end of 1983, with Anderson coaxed back into the band. (*Atco*)

Above: *9012Live The Solos*. An odd folly of a single live album, released to coincide with the similarly-named live VHS video. (*Atco*)

Left: Renewed interest during the 1980s led to a higher profile in the technical press, as seen here with Alan White on the cover of *Modern Drummer* magazine. (*David Watkinson Collection*)

Right: The vinyl cover of *Big Generator*, the band's laborious 1987 follow-up to *90125*. (*Atco*)

Left: The CD colour scheme for *Big Generator*, the first Yes album to get a simultaneous CD/ vinyl release. (*Atco*)

Right: *Anderson, Bruford, Wakeman, Howe*. Though not technically a Yes album, it certainly has the Yes 'spirit', even if some of the music betrays its origins as a Jon Anderson solo project. (*Arista*)

Left: *Union*. The album that brought ABWH and 'Yes West' together in an album that pleased almost nobody but still has a few decent moments. (*Arista*)

Right: The Suits Part One. Bill Bruford chats to Brian Lane, a former Yes and ABWH manager.

Left: The Suits Part Two. Phil Carson, the long-time Yes champion at Atlantic Records, who bankrolled the band through the Cinema era.

The Solo Albums

While the albums themselves – in terms of a track-by-track analysis at least – are beyond the scope of this book, it is worth looking at them in brief, since they represent two years in the history of the band.

The period from autumn 1974 to late summer 1976 represents a period of sporadic touring, mainly in the US. As often happens with a band of this apparent stature, riding a wave of excellent album sales, they made a joint decision – indulged by label Atlantic – to make solo albums, recorded around the touring, rather than rush into the studio (or maybe Squire's garage) and make another album with Moraz.

So, the five musicians, with occasional help from their bandmates, went their own separate ways to put their individual ideas onto vinyl. The whole process could have been a trainwreck, but actually, all five of the resultant albums have plenty of merit. Indeed, the process produced one classic album 'for the ages', two almost as good, an underrated gem and a misfire with plenty still to admire. But which is which?

Steve Howe – Beginnings

Released: November 1975
Chart placings: UK: 22, US: 63
First out of the gate at the end of 1975 was Howe's *Beginnings* album. The record has had a real kicking from Yes fans over the years due to the quality of Howe's vocals, and the overall poor standard of the song material. You will find no revisionism here (not yet, at least), sadly. The problem seems to be that the keys are at the top end of Howe's range as a lead vocalist, and the melodies that he is asking himself to sing would challenge any vocalist, let alone someone with as little experience as the guitarist. Only on the final song, 'Break Away From It All', does his singing work, since it is performed as choral vocals in a mainly instrumental piece.

There are several instrumental pleasures, however. The title track, orchestrated by Patrick Moraz, is a wonder, as is the jaunty 'The Nature Of The Sea'. Alan White and Bill Bruford also guest. Much better was to follow for Howe, thankfully, with an excellent 1979 follow-up in *The Steve Howe Album,* which led to a long, and at the time of writing, unbroken string of high-quality solo efforts.

Chris Squire – Fish Out Of Water

Released: December 1975
Chart placings: UK: 25, US: 69
Next out was Chris Squire's remarkable *Fish Out Of Water*, a flawed masterpiece if ever there was one. Yes fans always knew Squire could sing, and here he shows how adept he is as a lead vocalist. There's a LOT of bass on the album, as one might expect, but here it mainly serves that material, which is very good. Terrific support comes from Moraz (again), Bill Bruford

(who drums throughout and is terrific) and Andrew Pryce Jackman, whose orchestrations are exquisite.

If the album has a flaw, it's because, with only five songs in total, the two longer pieces arguably overstay their welcome. 'Silently Falling' is thrilling up to the seven-minute mark, and might have been better ending there, while album closer 'Lucky Seven', which closes as an orchestral canon, feels like it is ending around eight and a half minutes, yet builds again to another big finish. It's bold, certainly, but it doesn't quite work to these ears.

These flaws aside, it's terrific.

Alan White – Ramshackled

Released: March 1976

Chart placings: UK: 41, US: did not chart

White's album was the next to arrive. It's been the recipient of quite a bit of disdain from Yes fans for the cardinal sin of not being very progressive, so if any of the five solo albums is worthy of reappraisal (sorry, Steve), it's this one. True, its songs have a mid-1970s pop-soul vibe that has not worn especially well. But, on an album where most attention has gone on the sweet but inconsequential 'Spring-Song Of Innocence' simply due to the presence of Anderson and Howe, several tracks have gone relatively unloved. Try the poppy 'One Way Rag' or the fun big band jazz of 'Avakak' and the expansive pop-jazz of closer 'Darkness'.

White plays drums only, so most of the creativity lies in the hands of keyboard player Kenny Craddock and guitarist Pete Kirtley, who, it has to be said, do an excellent job. In short, don't believe the naysayers. Give the album a go yourself. You might be pleasantly surprised.

Patrick Moraz – The Story Of I

Released: April 1976

Chart placings: UK: 28, US: 132

Sometimes called just *Patrick Moraz,* this features no Yes members – past or present – but brings together top-of-the-range jazz-fusion players like bassist Jeff Berlin and drummer Alphonse Mouzon. The album also features the singing and songwriting talents of John McBurnie, who had previously been in Jackson Heights, a post-Nice project of Moraz's compatriot in Refugee, Lee Jackson.

The result is a bonkers but hugely endearing two sides of vinyl that mixes Brazilian rhythms with pop, prog and fusion. The production is a little flat, but even with that, it's terrific – if not for the faint-hearted. Moraz has gone on to a lengthy solo career, but only this and its post-Yes follow-up *Out In The Sun* have charted in the UK.

Jon Anderson – Olias Of Sunhillow

Released: July 1976

Chart placings: UK: 8, US: 47

Finally, we come to the most successful of the five albums and the longest in arriving. This completely unique album is one of a kind, created entirely within the imagination of the vocalist, and with every instrument played by him. As we know, Anderson's instrumental skills are fairly rudimentary, so his ability to record an album without other musicians severely restricted what he could play. But he really made it work for him. Based around a mystical fantasy storyline, Anderson's objective was to create an otherworldly musical construct. It challenged his mental health as he layered guitars, keyboards, percussion and vocals to create his vision. The results are astonishing – thoroughly progressive, yet not 'rock' as such. There are no kit drums, and the bass playing is rhythmic and rudimentary. The character of the piece comes from Anderson's tuneful writing, his chanted vocals and the wealth of keyboard and percussive textures. The album performed well in the UK, reaching the top ten.

Yes Live 1975 And 1976

Live 1975 At QPR

Recorded At Loftus Road, London. 10th May 1975
Released on Laserdisc in 2001
Tracklisting:
Disc One. 1.'Introduction - Igor Stravinsky: Firebird Suite/Sound Chaser' 2. 'Close to the Edge' 3.'To Be Over' 4.'The Gates of Delirium' 5. 'I've Seen All Good People: Your Move/Mood for a Day/Long Distance Runaround (Acoustic)/Clap'
Disc Two. 1. 'And You and I' 2.'Ritual' 3.'Roundabout' 4.'Sweet Dreams' 5.'Yours Is No Disgrace'
Total running time: 148 minutes

Aside from some bootlegs of variable quality, we have three main documents of Yes live during the Patrick Moraz era. The first is *Live 1975 At QPR.* This was a rare concert at the Loftus Road football stadium. Part of this lengthy performance was broadcast on the BBC's *Old Grey Whistle Test,* and has a decent mix, whereas a good portion of the concert, while filmed by the BBC, was not broadcast and was never mixed, so the audio seems to be a monitor mix, which – frustratingly – gives an impression of the concert audio rather than a correct mix of it. Nonetheless, it's an impressively complete document of the Yes show at the time.

The UK tour had begun in April of that year, with the band playing all of *Relayer*, as you might expect, plus 'Close To The Edge' and 'And You And I'. Tellingly, the only piece from *Topographic Oceans* played was an extended 'Ritual', complete with the ultra-visual percussion extravaganza. Despite its flaws, it made for an impressive set closer, as it also did on the 2004 world tour.

Overall, it's a great show, with Moraz's re-interpretations of some of the keyboard parts made more familiar by Wakeman and Kaye a particular delight. Also notable when watching, rather than listening, are Anderson's attempts at instrumentation, especially the tin whistle in 'Sound Chaser' and some surprisingly effective, albeit scratchy, rhythm guitar in 'Gates Of Delerium'.

Roosevelt Stadium, Jersey City, 17 June 1976

Released: July 2026
Label: Rhino
Produced by Eddie Offord and Yes
Tracklisting:
1. 'Apocalypse', 2. 'Siberian Khatru', 3. 'Sound Chaser', 4. 'The Gates Of Delirium', 5. 'I've Seen All Good People', 6. 'Long Distance Runaround', 7. 'Patrick Moraz Solo', 8. 'Clap', 9. 'Harp Solo', 10. 'Ritual', 11. 'Heart Of The Sunrise', 12. 'Roundabout', 13. 'I'm Down'

Available as a bootleg for many years, this show, recorded 13 months later during the band's summer tour for radio broadcast, was finally given a decent wash and brush-up and released in July 2026.

Even then, some fans with no idea of historical context weren't happy. But actually, given the source, it sounds great, and it's another great document for the band at this point in their history.

By the summer of 1976, most (but not all, Anderson's had yet to appear) of the band's solo albums had been released, and at the beginning of the tour each member had showcased some of those albums. Within a couple of weeks, however, the full band versions had been dropped, with 'Ritual' hastily reinstated. A look at those early setlists tells a sobering story. The initial sets are so packed with solo material that one wonders how they could possibly have worked for an audience. It's clear they didn't.

By mid-June, the set had a much better balance. Each band member had a solo moment, although Squire and White's were both in 'Ritual'. In a ten-minute solo section, Moraz's solo incorporated moments from *The Story Of I,* Howe bashed off 'Clap' and Anderson played a harp solo with melodic assistance from Moraz, incorporating moments from *Olias Of Sunhillow,* but these are better off seen as solos (or a duet in the latter case) rather than 'excerpts from…', despite the track titles on the album cover.

There were some other changes to the 1975 sets. In a shorter set overall, probably due to the presence of other artists on these multi-band outdoor concerts, 'Siberian Khatru' replaced the other two pieces from *Close To The Edge,* and a searing 'Heart Of The Sunrise' came back in for the first time since 1972, with some interesting electronics from Moraz.

'To Be Over' from *Relayer* had also been dropped by this point. It's a delicate piece and not always at its best in a live environment, as Steve Howe explained to the author in 2025, when asked about playing it live in the future.

> It's one of a few Yes pieces where I'm not totally sure how we'd pull that off on stage. It has a studio dynamic, with Alan White playing very softly and in a laid-back way. But it also has some dramatic moments. I'd wonder how to get the pedal steel loud enough in the mix, which is a key thing I did on the record that I love very much. But to capture the dynamics of the song would be extremely challenging.

Yesshows
Released: December 1980
Label: Atlantic
Full credits when the album is discussed more fully

Two pieces from the era wound up on *Yesshows*, released in 1980. The versions of 'Gates' and 'Ritual' stem from two months later (17 August) at The Cobo Arena in Detroit, and are not dissimilar to the versions on *Roosevelt Stadium*. Sonically, they are better, and Anderson is pleasingly shouty on 'Gates', but the mixes are a touch flatter. Which versions are better? It's marginal stuff.

Going For The One (1977)

Personnel:
Jon Anderson: vocals, harp
Chris Squire: bass, vocals
Steve Howe: electric and acoustic guitar, pedal steel, vocals
Alan White: drums, tuned percussion
Rick Wakeman: keyboards, piano, polymoog, church organ
The Richard Williams Singers: choir
Produced at Mountain Studios, Montreux, Switzerland, by Yes from October 1976 to April 1977
Engineer: John Timperley, assisted by David Richards
Executive producer: Brian Lane
Released: July 1977
Highest chart places: UK: 1, US: 8
Running time: 38:49

By the time the band, including Patrick Moraz, returned to the studio to record their next album, it had been two years since *Relayer*. All five members had released their solo albums, and there had been two long – and lucrative – summer tours, mainly playing stadiums and arenas in the US. Choosing to record in Switzerland – Moraz's home country – for tax reasons must have been thrilling for him, yet within a few weeks, he was out of the band.

Supposedly, he wasn't gelling musically, yet there is also a suggestion of manoeuvring by Brian Lane, manager both of the band and Rick Wakeman. Lane's executive producer credit is no coincidence, and nor, one suspects, was Wakeman's reinstatement following the recent dip in his solo career.

With Rick back as a 'session player', initially, at least, the first question often asked is 'how much Moraz is on the album?' This is impossible to answer; he certainly has no writing credits, yet Moraz lays claim to a big part of the initial development of the arrangements for the songs, which is likely. With Wakeman back and enthusiastic about the more concise, melodic approach evident in the music, there were other changes, too.

Eddie Offord was out, replaced by engineer John Timperley, best known for his 1960s work with Cream and The Beatles. The band self-produced. Gone also was Roger Dean, with the album given a striking, modern cover by Hipgnosis. Frankly, although the cover, with a naked man looking up at angular, skyscraper-style objects against a blue sky (or blue background, at least), is hard to forget, it has dated very badly compared to the timeless surrealism of Dean's early 1970s covers, many of which are still considered iconic today.

Containing three pieces broadly considered 'songs', a longer, more esoteric piece in 'Turn Of The Century' and the 15-minute 'Awaken', the album itself has a reputation as a masterpiece: the last 'great' Yes album. It is hard to disagree, yet it does have its frustrations. Offord is badly missed, and the final mix seems very thin, even on the remastered Rhino version, and it is drenched in reverb. That it is considered a great album despite this fundamental flaw demonstrates the quality of the material, the arrangements and the playing. Like the best Yes albums, what makes *Going For The One* really special is the unique atmosphere it creates. There is no other album like it, and it's hard to compare its individual five tracks with anything else in the catalogue. Its reputation has also been enhanced because it is so well thought of by the band itself, deemed by all concerned a happy experience, with Wakeman's eventual return as a full-time member the icing on the cake.

Largely well-received by the press on its release, the album performed well, reaching number one in the UK album charts, without reaching the massive worldwide status of *Fragile* or *Close To The Edge*, and was assisted in the UK at least by the rather unexpected success of 'Wonderous Stories' – a top ten hit single in 1977.

'Going For The One' (Anderson)

The band go for the jugular from the first moment with some searing pedal steel guitar from Steve Howe, an unusual usage of this instrument more regularly associated with country music. The riffing at the start of the second verse is particularly impressive. Wakeman has fun with a funky piano part. Still, otherwise, it's Anderson's song, an extended 'horse racing' metaphor leading into a fairly obvious dig at his 'hippy-dippy' public image and the difficulty of coming up with lyrics.

Despite the aggression of the track, there's still time for plenty of Yes-ish subtlety, with a 'Siberian Khatru' word list, some dancing bass and some inventive backing vocals from Squire, and the sort of drumming from White that would never have been contemplated in the Bruford era. A good piece played live, as you might expect, it has dropped in and out of the band's set over the last 40 years. Its lack of ubiquity may possibly be due to its relative brevity.

'Turn Of The Century' (Anderson, Howe, White)

Struggling with the emotional angst of being 16, this was probably my favourite song by the band for a long time. Lyrically, and tonally, this delightful piece of music is shamelessly romantic, even for Anderson, never one to hold back on his feelings.

It tells the age-old story of a man who loses his love to mortality, and is compelled to reproduce her in sculpture, only to find his passion animating the statue. It is one of those pieces where the instrumentation enhances the story perfectly, building tension and release at exactly the right moments.

Howe's classical guitar at the start is beautiful, and Anderson's reverb-heavy vocal pulls at the heartstrings, with Wakeman's keyboards subtle and distant, joined by some delicate percussion from White and Squire's backing vocals. Halfway through, Wakeman's piano takes over, joined by Howe's guitar and

Squire's bass, with White switching to timpani. At one point, at around 5.05, the arrangement almost trips up on itself, but then the instruments come together in unison, building to the final, hugely uplifting vocal section before ending on Howe's classical guitar once again.

A difficult piece to pull off live, the song has never been a regular part of the live set but has made a few appearances on the 2004 world tour and as part of the 1996 *Keys To Ascension* concerts.

'Parallels' (Squire)

Only Yes would attempt an entire track with the band rocking out and Wakeman playing only one instrument: a huge church organ recorded at St. Martin's Church, Vevey in Switzerland. That the band could achieve this – he played over a high-speed phone line – is thanks to the Swiss's technological sophistication. This was 1976, let us not forget. As a song, this rocker from Chris Squire is powerful stuff, including some wonderful lead guitar from Howe. Wakeman's church organ is certainly worth the effort, giving the track a tone hard to achieve on the Hammond, and the organ 'break' in the middle of the song is very effective. Howe can't have traded lead lines with such an instrument very often. The three-part vocal towards the end of the song – with Squire on the left, Anderson in the middle and Howe on the right – is also very effective.

Despite being a big, rocking track, 'Parallels' hasn't been played live very often, probably because it's hard to replicate the church organ sound on a Hammond. When the band performed it on the *Going For The One* tour – when it opened the show – Wakeman played his mid-song solo on Minimoog, to really good effect, as can be heard on the *Yesshows* live album.

'Wonderous Stories' (Anderson)

A top ten hit single in the UK, this delicate and tuneful piece is a delightfully evocative song from Anderson. Howe plays the Leode, last heard on 'Your Move', and Wakeman solos effectively on Polymoog, an early polyphonic synth also beloved of Tony Banks of Genesis. Like 'Turn Of The Century', this song shows how well Yes could do 'delicate' even playing as a full band, although there are no drums on this studio version. It is a perfectly constructed three minutes and 50 seconds. Something of a throwaway track in a live setting, it has popped in and out of the live set on a regular basis, with the band feeling no obligation to play it on every tour, unlike 'Owner Of A Lonely Heart', despite its hit status in the UK.

'Awaken' (Anderson, Howe)

While *Going For The One* rarely wins 'Yes greatest album' polls, the track that tends to come first every time is this 15-and-a-half-minute masterpiece, which shows off everything that makes Yes, and indeed progressive rock, so compelling when it is done well. It has its neo-classical moments, particularly

Wakeman's piano introduction and also the slow build of the church organ in the instrumental middle part. But it's a masterpiece of construction, from the ensemble virtuosity of the opening full-band section, with Howe and Wakeman in complete harmony (unlike *Tormato*).

Howe, once again, is in astonishing form, as he is throughout the album, and here the church organ is integrated amongst the other instruments before coming into its own during the slow build of percussion, organ and Anderson's harp. The choir is also a masterstroke, sung by The Richard Williams Singers with an arrangement by Rick Wakeman. There is huge tension in this mid-section, as the rest of the band enter gradually against Wakeman's church organ, first Squire's bass, then Howe's delicate electric guitar, building as White switches back to drums and Anderson sings the 'Master Of Images' section. The piece continues to build in intensity towards the final, ecstatic 'Like The Time I Ran Away' section and Howe's final electric guitar coda.

'Awaken' is an incredibly effective live piece, and a powerful set closer. On *The Ladder* tour, the band sometimes showered the audience with ticker tape, as shown on the live DVD, but again there are many live recordings to choose from, and, like 'And You And I', it is a real show-stopper. Although some compromises were needed to rearrange the track to be played live, few liberties had been taken with the arrangement overall until, that is, Yes – featuring Anderson, Rabin, Wakeman – put in some effective percussion-based embellishments into their otherwise faithful rendition during 2017 and 2018.

Related Tracks

'Montreux's Theme' (Howe, Squire, Anderson, White)
A rather aimless but pleasant, almost jazzy instrumental dominated by Howe, with Anderson (by the sound of it) on rhythm guitar and barely any keyboards except possibly some organ in the background.

'Vevey' (Anderson, Wakeman)
Anderson on (slightly hamfisted) harp and Wakeman on church organ improvise a few tunes. The organ is lovely. The harp is less so. The section on the Rhino re-master is rather better than the two snippets on the *Yesyears* boxed set. This is definitely 'listen once' music.

'Amazing Grace' (trad., arranged Squire)
A part of Squire's bass solo on some tours, this is a straight version of the main melody of the traditional hymn, played on an overdriven bass guitar and bass pedals. As a track in its own right, it's a bit pointless.

Tormato (1978)

Personnel:
Jon Anderson: vocals, Alvarez 10-string guitar
Chris Squire: Rickenbacker bass, bass pedals, piano, Gibson Thunderbird bass, vocals
Steve Howe: Les Paul Custom, Martin 00045, Gibson 'the Les Paul', Spanish Guitar, Fender Broadcaster, Mandolin, Gibson 175D, vocals
Alan White: drums, percussion, drum synthesizer
Rick Wakeman: Birotron, Hammond Organ, Polymoog, Harpsichord, piano, RMI computer keyboard
Damion Anderson: vocal on 'Circus Of Heaven'
Arranged and produced by Yes
Engineers: Geoff Young and Nigel Luby
Orchestral arrangement on 'Onward' and string arrangement on 'Madrigal' by Andrew Pryce Jackman
Recorded at Advision. Additional recording and mixing at RAK Studios, February to June 1978.
Executive producer: Brian Lane
Released: September 1978.
Highest chart places: UK: 8, US: 10
Running time: 41:35

Given its status in most polls as one of the poorer Yes albums, *Tormato* holds some sort of mythical status amongst a set minority of Yes fans. It was well-favoured enough to warrant its own book by *Yes Music Podcast* head honcho Kevin Mulryne, whose excellent tome, *Yes: The Tormato Story*, was published in 2023. Oliver Wakeman (who will feature in the next volume of our story) cites it as his favourite Yes album, and while there is no doubt it's 'problematic', there is much to its story that makes its creation and release far more interesting to Yes aficionados than more harmonious releases, such as the one that preceded it.

As for your author, *Tormato* was my 'entry' album to Yes. I saw the band live for the first time at Wembley Arena one month after the album's release, and it still holds a special place in my heart. And yet I have often wondered how the harmonious band that recorded and toured *Going For The One* began to sour so quickly. Despite some personal sentimental value, the album remains hugely flawed. Why?

Many commentators have rightly pointed out a problem with some of the arrangements on *Tormato*: Steve Howe and Rick Wakeman seem to be clashing and fighting for the same space in the mix. For the first time on a Yes album, both musicians had equal status in the band. On *Fragile* and *Close To The Edge*, Wakeman was a junior member in a developing band, while on *Topographic Oceans*, when he might have played a fuller part (when, ironically, he was given a one-fifth writing credit on the whole album), he was not fully engaged in the material presented by Howe and Anderson.

On *Going For The One*, he was a hired hand, adding fairy dust to already-established material. But here he was, a big star and part of a band as an equal member. He was entitled to his share of the limelight. This means that with no long pieces in the style of 'Awaken', some tracks were over-filled with Howe and Wakeman soloing against each other.

The album is also held up as an example of how not to self-produce, suggesting that the 'many hands on the fader' approach produced a lot of compromises and an overly compressed sound mix. Certainly, the mix has a compressed, cluttered feel, more in need of a remix than the earlier, classic albums so expertly and sensitively handled by Steven Wilson, although it is believed that the original multi-track recordings may be unavailable. This is not helped by some rather dated sounds, from the 'alien' effects in 'Arriving UFO' to Alan White's syn-drum in 'Release, Release'. Although the idea that punk and new wave thrust progressive rock aside is a myth, it is also clear that Atlantic were keen to receive a rockier album with briefer songs to take advantage of the changing market. To a certain extent, they got it.

Rick Wakeman was also favouring two keyboard instruments that were to become obsolete fairly quickly. The first was the Polymoog, an early polyphonic synthesizer manufactured until 1980. Wakeman was an early adopter of this instrument, understandably so as he has a close association with the Moog organisation, yet in this case, he backed the wrong horse, with Sequential Circuits' Prophet 5 and 10 becoming the more ubiquitous analogue polyphonic instruments in the late 1970s and early 1980s, before digital synthesizers took hold of the market.

The other instrument used extensively on *Tormato* was the Birotron, an advanced version of the Mellotron. Again, Wakeman was directly involved in the development of this instrument, which, while certainly innovative and a huge advance on the Mellotron, suffered from rapidly escalating costs so that, in the end, only a few were ever manufactured.

And yet there is still much to admire in *Tormato*. At its heart, the album is saved by some excellent songwriting – in this aspect, it is probably an advance on *Going For The One* – and some very fine playing from the band.

So, while it will never be considered a classic by all but a small proportion of Yes fans, it is far from the disaster it is often cracked up to be.

'Future Times' (Anderson, Howe, Squire, Wakeman, White)/**'Rejoice'** (Anderson)

Often held up as one of the tracks on which Howe and Wakeman clash, 'Future Times' is certainly a busy piece, with Squire's harmonised bass also fighting for attention. In the opening instrumental section, before the vocals arrive, Howe's Les Paul and Wakeman's Polymoog weave around each other. In another universe, one of these lines – probably Wakeman's synth – might have been ditched without causing any damage to the track at all. However, I think the arrangement actually works pretty well, with both instruments often in unison. If anything, at just over four minutes, it is too short.

Squire's bass in 'Rejoice' hints – and it is only a hint – at reggae, but the rest of the track is a showcase for Wakeman's synthesizer work. Both these short pieces are full of excellent ideas, dispensed with much too quickly. The band played these songs early in the set on the 1978-1979 *Tormato* world tour, and Jon Anderson took the reggae influence in 'Rejoice' and accentuated it when he played the song in his Yes medley on the *Song Of Seven* solo tour in 1980.

'Don't Kill The Whale' (Anderson, Squire)

Mainly penned by Squire, and presented to the band as a finished piece, this is a fairly straightforward song with a worthy, ecological subject. Howe's Les Paul is again prominent, and the Birotron can be heard on the verses in all its compressed glory. The band have played this live occasionally, particularly in the 2010s. It was a minor hit in the UK, reaching number 36 before the album's September 1978 release. Anderson also played a rearrangement of the song (combined with Led Zeppelin's 'Kashmir' of all pieces) on his tours with the Paul Green Rock Academy in 2022 and 2023.

'Madrigal' (Anderson, Wakeman)

Rick Wakeman's excursions on harpsichord are rare but always excellent. Utterly charming, this simple piece features Wakeman on the instrument and Steve Howe playing Spanish guitar. Add to that a typically 'out there' lyric from Anderson and some beautiful harmony vocals, and that's all you need, really. One of Yes' most delightful short pieces, it was played live during 1978, and also by the 2020s lineup as a 'deep cut'. For more details on the harpsichord the band used, see Kevin Mulryne's book.

'Release, Release' (Anderson, White, Squire)

Yes have never been afraid to 'rock out', even prior to the Rabin era. However, for the five and a half minutes of 'Release, Release', they showed that even they could play with blues chords once in a while. The song is an up-tempo rocker, driven by some terrific drumming from Alan White, and dominated by Steve Howe's Fender Broadcaster, his weapon of choice on *Relayer*. However, it is the Yes trademark – inventive, beautifully crafted vocal arrangements – that are most impressive here. Only Wakeman's Polymoog soloing, pretty much throughout the early verses, seems out of place. The drum solo/fake crowd noise section is an interesting (if controversial) touch; though it leads into a guitar solo, it does build some tension before the 'straight jacket, freedom's march' vocal section. Wakeman is better used during his solo late in the song. Powerful and exuberant, this is, in the main, terrific stuff, perhaps a precursor of the rockier approach to be found two years later on *Drama*. Ironically, for a song that begs to be played live, it was dropped quite early on in 1978 as the vocals were too high for Anderson to sing without putting unnecessary pressure on his voice.

'Arriving UFO' (Anderson, Howe, Wakeman)
Another track played live occasionally on the *Tormato* tour but completely ignored, since it's rather quirky and dated. Riffing on the then-current craze for all things extraterrestrial, heralded by Steve Spielberg's *Close Encounters Of The Third Kind*, the tone of this piece also suggests 'Teakbois' from *Anderson, Bruford, Wakeman, Howe* 11 years later, a track that is equally derided. Both Wakeman's Polymoog chords and Alan White's syn drums have dated quite badly. Amongst the silliness – and I remember we thought it a bit silly even at the time – is some terrific bass from Chris Squire and a great Les Paul solo from Howe that deserves to be on a better piece of music. Again, if you must delve a little more deeply into this interesting but rather silly piece, Kevin Mulryne's book will tell you all you need to know.

'Circus Of Heaven' (Anderson)
Speaking of silly, the quirkiness continues with this cloying piece of kitsch Bossa Nova, with hints of The Beatles, from the pen of Jon Anderson. Such high-concept music is difficult to pull off, and even the band's inventive playing cannot save it. Jon's son Damion provides the spoken word section at the end. The song was played live in 1978 and 1979.

'Onward' (Squire)
Another big shift in tone heralds this beautiful, romantic tune from Squire. Although a million miles from the early 1970s Yes sound, it remains a minor classic. It took on new meaning in the wake of Squire's death in 2015, as the band played it on tape at the start of shows, a single spotlight shining on his Rickenbacker as a tribute to their departed colleague. The song is a triumph of simplicity, with an orchestral arrangement from Andrew Pryce Jackman and an unusual guitar line from Howe, which complements Squire's rising and falling bassline perfectly. Anderson – as usual – sings like he means every moment and Squire himself also provides one of his most charming harmony vocals – a perfect illustration of why his voice blended so well with Anderson's.

'On The Silent Wings Of Freedom' (Anderson, Squire)
Squire is also heavily featured on the album's final eight-minute track, possibly the album's strongest 'full band' piece, soloing over some great drumming from White, while both Howe and Wakeman embellish inventively. While the song itself would not survive the 1978-1979 tour, until revived in a somewhat truncated and perhaps unsatisfactory form in 2022, Squire's bass riff would appear in the 'White-Fish' duo section of shows for many years to come. The slow atmospheric section before the final build towards the

album's powerful climax is the best calling card for the Birotron on the album and leads into Wakeman's strongest moment – an extended and thrilling Polymoog solo.

It's an effective end to a somewhat disjointed album.

Related Tracks

'Abilene' (Howe)

A rather turgid, throwaway pop song written by Steve Howe, which feels like a demo fleshed out quickly when an extra song was needed. Howe solos nicely, but the rest of the band appear disinterested. The song was the B-side of the 'Don't Kill The Whale' single.

'Money' (Squire, Anderson, White, Wakeman)

More throwaway stuff, this time a piece of good-time boogie during which Rick Wakeman performs an almost unintelligible impersonation of Denis Healey, then Chancellor of the Exchequer in the Labour government, which lasts, somewhat tortuously, for the entire song.

Yes Live In 1978 And 1979

Yes stayed on tour promoting *Tormato* for almost a year. This was not the fiery Yes of 1972, but a sleeker, more refined version of the band. Much of the improvisation had been replaced by slick, beautifully conceived arrangements, with the band playing a two-plus-hour set in the round, using a revolving stage that sometimes led to intriguing technical issues.

The setlist was well crafted to showcase some of the stronger tracks from *Tormato*, with 'The Big Medley', the only time the band have tried something of that sort, even if it was less a medley and more of a group of songs played together without stopping into one 26-minute sequence. Songs played were: 'Time And A Word', 'Long Distance Runaround', 'Survival' (a tiny excerpt), 'The Fish', 'Perpetual Change' and 'Soon'. There was also an interesting take on 'I've Seen All Good People' with little band solos at the end, and – famously – the best live version of 'Starship Trooper' to never be released, featuring two superb Wakeman Moog solos.

There are bootlegs, of course, and the poor quality *Live In Philadelphia* DVD, which does actually include 'Starship Trooper', although the whole thing has a reverb-heavy mix that doesn't show it at its best.

What, then, of the famed BBC broadcast from *The Friday Rock Show*? Many Yes fans have this – either from *Forgotten Yesterdays* or from the original broadcast – and while a few tracks have been used for *Yesshows* and the *Classic Yes* compilation, it's never seen the light of day. A semi-bootleg was offered for sale in 2025 but was withdrawn. Long-term Yes supporter Jon Dee is working on a restoration of the show, adding in the tracks the BBC edited out to get it down to two hours. At the time of writing, a release date had not been announced, but this author, for one, can't wait!

The Paris Sessions And Related Tracks (1979)

Personnel:
Jon Anderson: vocals, guitar
Chris Squire: bass, vocals
Steve Howe: guitars, vocals
Alan White: drums, percussion
Rick Wakeman: keyboards
Produced by Roy Thomas Baker
Recorded in Paris in autumn 1979

Following the in-the-round tour of 1978-79, the band took a short break and then convened in Paris with the famed – some might even say notorious – Roy Thomas Baker, best known for his work with Queen, producing them. The sessions did not go well, with the band factionalised into Howe, Squire and White versus Anderson and Wakeman.

Recording broke up before Christmas when White broke his foot roller skating. As the resulting tracks remained unreleased for many years, except for bootleg versions, they have received far more attention than they frankly deserve. We will add to the column inches here by briefly discussing the versions that were finally released.

What is clear is that the tracks we have are very Anderson/Wakeman-heavy, with some lacklustre bass and drums, and so little Howe that he may as well not be in the band. Indeed, Howe is almost entirely absent, but that may be down to his customary habit of recording his guitar parts separately. Or he hated the material. Or both. It is hard to know whether any of these songs might have been salvageable, but you can almost feel the boredom and animosity, giving the pieces a sort of macabre fascination. The writing credits shown are the 'official' ones, although it's more likely that most were written by Anderson and Wakeman only.

'Dancing Through The Light' (Anderson, Howe, Squire, Wakeman, White)
Source: Rhino remaster of Drama
Yes go disco! I guess that was inevitable, given that everyone was going a bit disco around that time. This rudimentary piece was the inspiration for the *Drama* track 'Dance Through The Light', and you can certainly hear it in this version, which contains no guitar and a vocoder-style vocal. Squire's bass is actually rather well done, even if White sounds a bit less comfortable with the disco style – he's solid in a rock sort of way. This isn't awful, but it's not much more than a demo.

'Golden Age' (Anderson, Howe, Squire, Wakeman, White)
Source: Rhino remaster of Drama
Again, a piece with some promise, but this sounds like a demo produced by Anderson and Wakeman, and the song itself doesn't really hang together. The

drums and bass don't sound convincing, and the guitar certainly sounds like Anderson rather than Howe. Wakeman used some of his parts for his *Rock 'N' Roll Prophet* album, while Anderson used other parts for 'Some Are Born' on his *Song Of Seven* solo album.

'Tango' (Anderson, Howe, Squire, Wakeman, White)
Source: In A Word boxed set
The tango-inspired verse is a terrible idea, but when the track leaps into life, it's not bad at all. Anderson's vocal is clearly a guide one only. This is another piece that might have been developed into something decent, and, again, it is Wakeman-heavy, with no guitar.

'In The Tower' (Anderson, Howe, Squire, Wakeman, White)
Source: Rhino remaster of Drama
An almost ecclesiastical organ backs a rather aimless Anderson melody, with some lacklustre drums and no bass or guitar to speak of. It's a demo and little more than that.

'Friend Of A Friend' (Anderson, Howe, Squire, Wakeman, White)
Source: Rhino remaster of Drama
Again, this is somewhat aimless stuff that might have developed into something more interesting. At least the whole band seems to be playing on this one, even if it's pretty rough and there's only rhythm guitar on it. There's a nice Wakeman keyboard run towards the end, but I'm clutching at straws, really.

'Never Done Before' (Anderson, Howe, Squire, Wakeman, White)
Source: In A Word boxed set
If in trouble, try to sound like The Beatles. Again, this has a nice honky-tonk piano solo from Wakeman and nothing else of note. Howe is again present, but only just.

A version of 'Everybody Loves You', which wound up on Anderson's solo album *Song Of Seven* in splendid shape, is also available on some bootlegs but has never been released officially.

Tormato Outtakes

The Rhino *Tormato* remaster contains a number of pieces of varying professionalism and quality, most likely additional songs recorded at RAK Studios after the main sessions at Advision had been completed for that album. Other versions of tracks like 'Money' have been released on bootlegs, though they offer very little extra information, and only the officially released versions are dealt with here. Some of these songs are clearly demos and may have been recorded at the composer's home.

'Picasso' (Anderson)
Source: Rhino remaster of Tormato
This is slight but rather lovely, and the whole band sound as though they mean it, so this probably comes from the *Tormato* sessions.

'Some Are Born' (Anderson)
Source: Rhino remaster of Tormato
An early but very recognisable version of the song that finally appeared on *Song Of Seven*. It is not as concise as the final version, but the bare bones are there.

'You Can Be Saved' (Squire)
Source: Rhino remaster of Tormato
A nice song from Squire, presented here in rudimentary form, sung as an untidy duet between Anderson and Squire.

'High' (Howe)
Source: Rhino remaster of Tormato
A rough-as-old-boots song from Howe – basically a riff with some sketchy vocals and drums. The guitar sounds for all the world like it's trying to play 'Heartsong' by guitarist Gordon Giltrap, but hearing Jon Anderson sing in the bath might be better than this.

'Days – Demo' (Anderson)
Source: Rhino remaster of Tormato
An *a capella* version of the piece that ended up on *Song Of Seven*. It actually works nicely sung like this.

'Countryside' (Anderson, Howe, Squire, White)
Source: Rhino remaster of Tormato
This is not bad, actually, thanks to the strength of the guitar part that underpins it. It was reworked as 'Corkscrew' for the Steve Howe album *Turbulence*, and was all the better for it.

'Everybody's Song' (Anderson, Howe, Squire, White)
Source: Rhino remaster of Tormato
This is basically the instrumentation of 'Does It Really Happen' from *Drama* with a sketch of an entirely different song from Anderson placed over the top. It's interesting to hear what might have been..

'Richard' (Anderson, Howe, Squire, Wakeman, White)
Source: In A Word boxed set
One of the era's better pieces, it actually sounds finished, if not particularly exciting, and it's not surprising that it didn't see the light of day until 2002.

'Crossfire' (Squire, Howe)
Source: In A Word boxed set
Presumably, an unused Howe/Squire/White trio piece from the *Drama* sessions, although it may be from Paris. Tonally, it's not really in keeping with the rest of the material on the album, but it's rather promising nonetheless.

Above: A publicity shot from the *Drama* era. (*Atlantic*)

Drama (1980)

Personnel:
Trevor Horn: vocals, bass
Chris Squire: bass, piano, vocals
Steve Howe: guitar, vocals
Alan White: drums, percussion, vocals
Geoff Downes: keyboards and vocoder
Arranged and produced by Yes
Backing tracks produced by Eddie Offord
Recorded at the Town House, London, between April and June 1980
Engineer: Hugh Padgham
Mixed at Sarm Studios
Highest chart places: UK: 2, US: 18
Running time: 36:55

The early part of 1980 was another period of crisis for Yes. With the Paris Sessions of late 1979 suspended, the plan was that they would reconvene in the new year in London, when Alan White's foot injury had healed. This was a messy break-up, with Wakeman and Anderson making no attempts to return to London. Whether the pair formally left the band at this point is open to interpretation. In his autobiography, Steve Howe reports that Anderson did show up at the studio at one point and played the band some of the songs he had been working on. They were full of cheery choruses and major keys. Indeed, much of Anderson's solo album *Song Of Seven*, released later that year, consists of such songs, so Howe's comment rings true. Wakeman never showed at all.

As a result, with White recovered, the three remaining members continued rehearsing. Having the same management, Brian Lane, The Buggles were introduced to the band, consisting of Trevor Horn and Geoff Downes, who had had a massive UK hit in 1979 with their bubblegum novelty-pop classic 'Video Killed The Radio Star'. This had given them some fame, and their debut album, *The Age Of Plastic,* also contained some great songs amongst the futuristic techno-sheen.

To some, the collaboration (unkindly called 'Yuggles' by the nay-sayers) was a joke. A ridiculous meeting of old-school progressive gravitas and lightweight pop. Others, however, saw the truth of the matter. These were proper musicians with the right credentials and attitude. Hadn't people seen Downes's keyboard rig in the 'Video Killed The Radio Star' video? He was clearly a prog fan at heart, even if he did play in rubber gloves. In a Buggles video, at least. That Horn was a fine, talented musician and sang in a similar register to Jon Anderson was also helpful. Their introductory piece, 'We Can Fly From Here', was, and remains, a terrific song, although it failed to make it onto the resulting album, the band opting instead for their more collaborative pieces. However, they did pick apart a new Horn/Downes song, 'I am A Camera', for the terrific, epic 'Into The Lens'.

With the new Yes in place, the album's path did not run completely smoothly, with Eddie Offord arriving to produce, then departing fairly quickly, his eccentricity too much for everyone. This is a typical Yes move. When in crisis, the band returns to the mean. In this case, it meant hiring Eddie, the man so responsible for the success of everything from *The Yes Album* to *Relayer*. At the same time, the album also saw the first Roger Dean cover on a studio album since *Relayer*, even if, arguably, it wasn't his finest work.

With a (supposedly sell-out) tour booked for later in the year, the new band worked long hours to complete the album by June, with Steve Howe recording his guitar parts at RAK Studios without the band. Trevor Horn even got married, spending a weekend in Bournemouth rather than the exotic two-week honeymoon planned. But they got there.

The resulting album did fairly well commercially, reaching number two in Britain. Critics seemed to like it, too. It remains a band favourite, and after some hostility from fans to the lineup at the time, it seems to have gained in popularity since. Considering the chaos and speed with which the album was created, it is a remarkably powerful and cohesive effort. The 'power trio' of Howe, Squire and White are on stupendous form, seemingly unshackled once again by commercial considerations.

Howe, in particular, is remarkable, and with the battle between guitar and keyboards settled – Downes defers – he is allowed the space to produce his best work since *Relayer*. Horn fits in very well – on the album, at least – providing just enough Anderson-ness to offer comfort while also bringing plenty of his own personality. There are just hints of the popular genres at the time – heavy metal and new wave – but fundamentally, this is a great, powerful progressive rock album.

The eventful *Drama* tour saw Horn struggle with the Anderson material when tired and also receive a somewhat hostile reception from a small minority of UK audiences. The album had been somewhat repressed until the Benoît David/Jon Davidson era when 'Machine Messiah' and 'Tempus Fugit' were reintroduced into the set, culminating in full-album renditions during 2017 and 2018.

'Machine Messiah' (Horn, Downes, Squire, Howe, White)

Falsely accused of being 'heavy metal' on release by a press hungry to associate Yes with the current trends, to wit the 'New Wave Of British Heavy Metal', this superb piece does start with a heavy section, brought about by its deliberate, ponderous tone and White's powerful drumming, more than any overdriven guitars. Indeed, the verse has a lightness of touch and energy – not to mention a wonderful soaring guitar melody from Howe, plus some neo-classical organ and a synthesizer solo – all within the first four and a half minutes. This is all very Yes so far.

Whether by intent or design, the band also gradually introduce Horn as lead vocalist, with Squire very prominent in the opening salvos. Only during the atmospheric acoustic section do we realise that 'Yes have a new singer and he's actually ok!' 'Machine Messiah', written by the ensemble as a band pretty quickly, is a complete triumph. It offers no agenda. It isn't trying to shock (like 'Sound Chaser') or follow fashion (like 'Arriving UFO'); it looks back to *Fragile* and offers up a piece of well-structured, beautifully played progressive rock.

'Machine Messiah' was played on the *Drama* tour, but as you would expect, it was dropped when Anderson returned to the fold. When Benoît David was recruited in 2008, the band felt free to put it back in the set, and it became the centrepiece when *Drama* was performed in its entirety in 2017. It now has a place as a potential part of any set. It's been rehabilitated completely.

'White Car' (Horn, Downes, Squire, Howe, White)
Played mainly by Downes on the Fairlight keyboard, but with added instrumentation from Howe and White, this short piece is actually very effective as a palate cleanser after the bombast of 'Machine Messiah'. On the night I saw the band in London in 1980, it was played as an *a capella* piece at the end of the set as a tribute to John Lennon, who had just been killed in New York, much to the horror of the entire world.

'Does It Really Happen?' (Horn, Downes, Squire, Howe, White)
One of the tracks that the band were working on in Paris before Christmas 1979, this version gives the piece a makeover and shows that the band could still play with some complexity. Squire, in particular, holds the piece together with some astonishing bass playing.

Howe mainly plays rhythm here, with Downes allowed to shine on organ and synthesizer during the coda, and there are definitely shades of their future band Asia here. The coda also includes a proper bass solo from Squire. White shows off his mallet-percussion skills with what sounds like some nifty marimba.

'Into The Lens' (Horn, Downes, Squire, Howe, White)
This second proper 'epic' adapts the Buggles song 'I Am A Camera' and extends it in the Yes style. With choral voices being the main vocal tool on the first half of the album, the verses here give Horn his first extensive lead vocal. The 'and you, may find time will blind you' section, with Horn and Squire singing in harmony, is spine-tingling, and the whole piece is relentless – progressive rock played with the intensity of metal, with Howe soloing his heart out on both Fender Telecaster and his trusty pedal steel. One issue caused some Yes fans to baulk a little, namely the 'I am a Camera' hook, which some found too poppy to be Yes, made even worse when played on the Vocoder – but we all soon got over it. It's another terrific piece of music, beautifully constructed and executed.

'Run Through The Light' (Horn, Downes, Squire, Howe, White)
Probably the song that played most with what Yes were or could be, this piece has Horn playing fretless bass at Squire's insistence, one of only two times another musician has played bass on a Yes track, the other being Billy Sherwood on 'The More We Live, Let Go' from *Union*. His very different style is very impressive here on a song that owes a great deal, in this version at least, to The Police and the pop-reggae so popular around this time. Not that there's reggae here exactly, but the band certainly have fun with some rather more modern stylings. Indeed, a complete album sounding like this might have been interesting (if unlikely) had the lineup ventured back into the studio. The finished version is certainly an improvement on the first attempt recorded during The Paris Sessions, and the closing instrumental section is inspired, fading out too early.

'Tempus Fugit' (Horn, Downes, Squire, Howe, White)
The album finishes superbly with this powerful piece, based around Squire's harmonised bassline, one of his finest, played lightning fast. But there's more than bass to this astonishing, breathless five minutes. Each musician gels with each other while Downes' vocoder reminds us, triumphantly, which band we are listening to. This was the other piece re-introduced to the live set in the late 2000s, albeit played at a slightly less breakneck pace.

Trevor Horn also chose this song to sing when he guested with the band in 2016 and 2018, a bold choice considering how breathless a piece it is. But it's a superb close to a great album.

Related Tracks

'Have We Really Got To Go Through This' (Howe, Squire, White)
Source: The Rhino reissue of Drama
This is an up-tempo song – some might even consider it simple – with a distinct punk/new wave vibe. It was an instrumental piece the trio had been working on prior to the arrival of Horn and Downes.

'Go Through This' (Live)
Source: The Word Is Live boxed set
The piece above was finally worked into a full track and was played live on some dates of the *Drama* tour as a short, punky pop song. The rough version on the *Word Is Live* boxed set does it few favours, but you do get the gist.

'We Can Fly From Here' (Horn, Downes)
Source: The Word Is Live boxed set
We will talk about the song that Downes and Howe used as their calling card in the next book, but the only contemporary version by Yes is the live one on *The Word Is Live*, which shows how little it was tampered with when it was finally released in 2011.

'Song No. 4 (Satellite)' (Howe, Squire, White)
Source: The Rhino reissue of Drama
Another piece being worked on by the trio, it was never developed with Horn and Downes and so remains a promising backing track as far as Yes are concerned, although it was reworked as the song provisionally called 'Telephone Secrets' when Squire and White played with Jimmy Page in the short-lived XYZ project when Yes dissolved after the *Drama* tour.

'I Am A Camera' (Horn, Downes)
Source: The Buggles album Adventures In Modern Recording.
The bare bones of 'Into The Lens' made it onto The Buggles' second album, released in 1981, complete with drum machine, a lush, keyboard-based arrangement and some great bass from Horn. It's very 'Buggles' and also rather good.

Yesshows (1980)

Personnel:
Jon Anderson: vocals
Chris Squire: bass, vocals
Steve Howe: guitars, vocals
Alan White: drums
Rick Wakeman: keyboards except 'Ritual' and 'Gates Of Delirium'
Patrick Moraz: keyboards on 'Ritual' and 'Gates Of Delirium'
Recorded in 1976, 1977 and 1978
Mixed by Chris Squire at Sun Park Studios
Engineers: Geoff Young and Nigel Luby
Released: November 1980 on Atlantic Records
Highest chart placings: UK: 22, US: 43
Tracklist (on the 1994 CD version):
Disc One: 1. 'Parallels', 2. 'Time And A Word', 3. 'Going For The One', 4. 'The Gates Of Delirium'
Disc Two: 1. 'Don't Kill The Whale', 2. 'Ritual', 3. 'Wonderous Stories'
Additional songs on the 2009 reissue: 1. 'I've Seen All Good People', 2. 'Roundabout'

Given that it was eight years since the shows that made up *Yessongs* had been recorded, another Yes live album was certainly overdue. The shows from 1976 to 1978 (note: there's nothing from 1973 to 1975, a time during which the band played as many live shows as ever, including the *Tales* and initial *Relayer* shows) were compiled and mixed by Chris Squire and presented to the band, who felt they needed further work.

However, when the band fell apart after the ill-fated Paris Sessions, the mixes were left in limbo, but scheduled for release by Atlantic without consulting the band at the end of 1980, just as the *Drama* lineup were on tour in the UK.

There's good and bad here. The good news is that Squire's mixes are pretty decent, especially 'The Gates Of Delerium', which, while it loses some of Moraz's sound design, gains in power, especially from Anderson, who deploys his 'rock' voice to stunning effect. The performances are also excellent, although the version of 'Ritual' is a bit bloated and the percussion extravaganza is dull without actually being able to see the band hit things! Wakeman's Moog solo on 'Parallels' is superb, as is the florid arrangement of 'Time And A Word'. The sound quality, a few years on from the first live album, is also generally very good.

Of course, with only four sides of vinyl to play with, there are some omissions. It would have been great to hear 'Sound Chaser' or some lip service paid to *Tormato*. But the most notable issue is the omission of 'Awaken'. Although Squire must have felt that he had to represent *Topographic Oceans* somehow, and include 'Ritual', a more vinyl-friendly piece like 'Awaken' might have been a better bet.

Which leads us to the faux pas. There are two. First of all, while *Yesshows* is not the first album to have a piece that is too long for a side of vinyl to fade out and continue after the record has been flipped over, here it really jars. It was corrected for the CD reissue, thankfully. Secondly, there's a very odd edit. When the band played 'Time And A Word' live in 1978, it went directly into 'Long Distance Runaround' as part of 'The Big Medley'; here it jumps into 'Going For The One' from the tour before, which insults die-hard Yes fans, to be honest.

While the sum of its parts isn't really up to much of a coherent live album as a collection of pretty decent tracks, it's very nice to have.

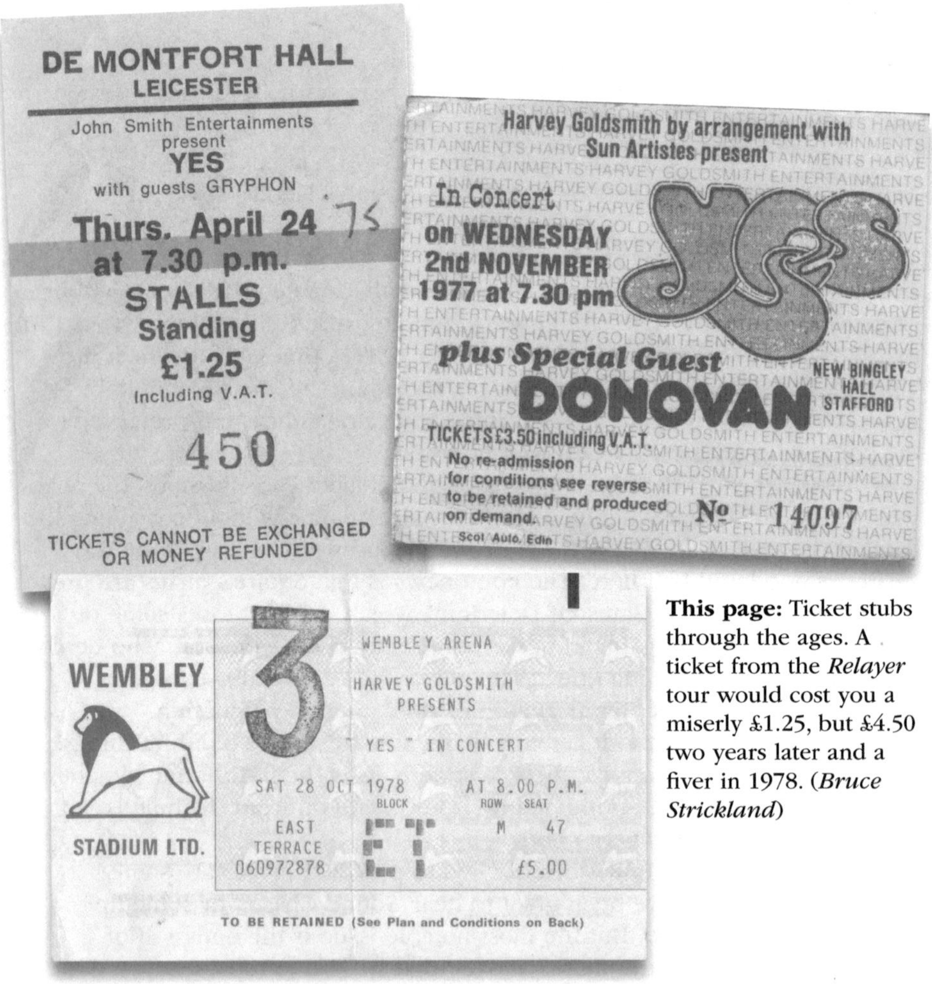

This page: Ticket stubs through the ages. A ticket from the *Relayer* tour would cost you a miserly £1.25, but £4.50 two years later and a fiver in 1978. (*Bruce Strickland*)

90125 (1983)

Personnel:
Jon Anderson: vocals
Chris Squire: bass, vocals
Trevor Rabin: guitar, keyboards, vocals
Alan White: drums, percussion, Fairlight, vocals
Tony Kaye: keyboards
Deepak Khazanchi: sitar and tambura on 'It Can Happen'
Graham Preskett: violin on 'Leave It'
Trevor Horn: backing vocals
Produced at Sarm Studios, London, between November 1982 and July 1983 by Trevor Horn
Julian Mendelson: additional engineer
Stuart Bruce: additional engineer
Jonathan Jeczalik: keyboard programming
Dave Lawson: keyboard programming
Keith Finney: assistant engineer
Released: November 1983
Highest chart places: UK: 16, US: 5
Running time: 44:49

At the end of the *Drama* tour in 1980, Yes seemed to be over as a band. Steve Howe and Geoff Downes formed Asia, Trevor Horn restarted his production career and Chris Squire and Alan White spent some months rehearsing a band with Led Zeppelin's Jimmy Page called XYZ. When that project stalled due to management difficulties, the pair were introduced to South African multi-instrumentalist Trevor Rabin via Phil Carson at Atlantic.

Rabin had released three well-received solo albums while living in the UK at the end of the 1970s but was now trying his luck in Los Angeles, where he had had a development contract with the Geffen label. This had not gone especially well – Rabin had tried out with Asia but had not enjoyed the experience. He was still touting around his songs, which included early versions of 'Owner Of A Lonely Heart' and ' Changes'. The three men jammed and gelled as a unit, and when Squire recruited Tony Kaye after they met each other socially, the four-piece band Cinema was born. For a while, at least.

The group rehearsed hard at John Henry rehearsal studio in Islington. This was something of a stop-start process, since Rabin and Kaye were Los Angeles residents stuck in London but, understandably, wanted to go home from time to time. But the material was honed gradually. Some work-in-progress recordings were made at Chris Squire's Sunpark Studio (at his home in Virginia Water, Surrey, where *Relayer* had been recorded) and appear on expanded versions of *90125*. They began an album with Trevor Horn producing at Sarm Studios (and various other studios around London) towards the end of 1982.

Two things should be noted at this point. The band had a development deal and an advance, but spent them quickly, so subsequent bankrolling was provided by Phil Carson himself. He even let Rabin and Kaye stay with him. Furthermore, at this stage the band had no record deal.

The recording went well, though Horn and Kaye did not see eye to eye, and eventually, quite late in the process, the keyboard player was back in Los Angeles. As Horn points out in his autobiography, it was never his intention to fire Kaye from the band, just from the session. This left Rabin with the task of completing the keyboard parts.

Furthermore, with Rabin and Squire slated to share lead vocal duties, there was some concern that the band was not strong enough vocally. Phil Carson suggested Jon Anderson as a possible singer, and despite some initial animosity between him and Squire, and some initial resistance from Rabin and White, he joined the project in the summer of 1983, very late in the recording process. The band became Yes again.

It's important to note that despite the development deal, Yes had no recording contract at this time. It wasn't until Carson tracked down Atlantic boss Ahmet Ertegun and played him 'Owner' that the band were finally offered a contract and Carson himself got all his investment money back.

Although it still has plenty of naysayers, *90125* is a really good album. Despite the 1980s production bells and whistles, it stands up well today. There are several reasons for this. Horn gave the band focus and concision; Rabin – as it turned out – was a first-rate musician and songwriter, albeit with a tendency to write and play within AOR conventions. As a result, the material is excellent throughout. The album has no filler, either; each track sounds fresh, different and well-crafted. But the thing that makes a good 'Cinema' album into a great Yes one is the sprinkling of fairy dust that Jon Anderson provides. His influence can be discerned in the number of writing credits he has – seven out of nine – an amazing feat considering how late he was recruited to the project. His contributions take the album to another level.

Tony Kaye is likely rarely to be found in the final mix. He certainly plays on 'Cinema' and 'Hearts'. Seemingly completely out of the band, Kaye was replaced by Eddie Jobson (of UK, Frank Zappa and the early 1980s Jethro Tull). Indeed, Jobson can be seen briefly in the video for 'Owner Of A Lonely Heart', and was involved in all the initial promotion for the album, although by the time the band were promoting the single, Kaye was back in the fold.

The timing, the good fortune of finding Anderson again, the huge success of 'Owner Of A Lonely Heart' and this new corporate rock era led to a new lease of life for the band, which, after a huge world tour in 1984 and early 1985, they messed up completely.

'Owner Of A Lonely Heart' (Rabin, Anderson, Squire, Horn)

There is no need to speculate a great deal about this most famous of tracks – a number one hit single in the US, of course – since Trevor Rabin's original demo is in the public domain and many comments by Rabin – and Trevor Horn in particular – are available. The demo is remarkably faithful to the finished version, although the verses and intro are more musically oriented towards AOR, which was Rabin's natural writing style.

Horn heard the demo accidentally while Rabin was in the bathroom during a listening session and liked much of the song. Realising that the chorus, in particular, was a winner, he begged the band to record the track, feeling that the album needed a single, not just for the sake of sales, but for his own rapidly-burgeoning 'hit maker' reputation. He describes a process where the band rehearsed the song over the course of a week while he struggled to keep their 'rock' affectations out of their arrangement. He rewrote the verses with Rabin, making them more concise, but allowed Jon Anderson to rewrite some of the words in the second verse. The gunshot after the 'eagle in the sky' lyric is Horn 'literally' shooting down the eagle. The famous horn stabs were added post-recording by Alan White, and the metronomic beat is provided not by programming alone but by manipulation of Alan White's snare drum, tuned to a top A.

But what of the origins of those Fairlight stabs? Chris Squire explained in the *Yes Classic Artists* documentary:

> Before Trevor [Horn] produced *90125*, the previous album he did was *Soweto* [actually *Duck Rock*], a Malcolm McLaren solo album. Malcolm went around all these clubs in New York where they were doing the scratching in the early days of rap with his cassette recorder. He was recording all these sounds and then, of course, they were used on his album, but they were all in the machine, so when we came to do our album, we said, 'let's have a look through Malcolm's library and see what we can use'. In fact, the James Brown horns were one of those samples [those famous horn stabs].

'Owner Of A Lonely Heart' is the first track to demonstrate one of the main features of the Rabin-era Yes albums – the contrast between the voices of Rabin and Anderson. Rabin has the smooth, AOR tones, while Anderson's schoolboy alto has more attack, and his delivery of the lead vocal here is the icing on the cake, lifting the song from the good to the great. Rabin's innovative guitar solo also impresses, with its use of a harmoniser pedal playing fifths, as does a nifty key change just before the fade-out. It was also a bold move to open the album with the track, very much a statement that this was a 'new' Yes.

Despite a couple of pretty terrible videos – readers might like to check out the alternative 'desert set' video (recorded for German TV) on YouTube to the more often seen 'dramatic'version – the quality of the song and Horn's remarkable production lifted it into the top 20 in 19 different territories. Only in the unforgiving UK market – where Yes were as unfashionable as a band could possibly be – did it disappoint, reaching number 28. So iconic has the song become, however, that it has had the remix treatment several times, most famously by Max Graham, who had a UK top ten hit with the track in 2012.

'Hold On' (Rabin/ Anderson/Squire) (5.18)

If, on buying the album, die-hard Yes fans were disturbed by 'Owner', their fears were unlikely to be allayed by the track that's up next: the swinging, swaggering stadium rocker 'Hold On'. This was compiled from two different Rabin songs that happened to be in the same tempo (and, indeed, have some similarities in their verses): 'Moving In' and 'Hold On'. The riff and verse melodies were taken from the former and the chorus (with some slight melodic variations) from the latter. I rather like the chorus of 'Moving In'; having said that, it's a shame Rabin never repurposed it.

'Hold On' is big, loud and bold; not in a metallic way, but more in an old-school classic rock style. The verses are sung in harmony by Anderson and Squire (and sound fantastic). It's clear that Anderson rewrote the verse lyrics completely, bringing in his main lyrical theme for the album, which is broadly 'find your own truth in the madness', a much wider and more political subject than Rabin's more personal lyrics, which discussed his own situation circa 1981. Squire has some of his best swooping bass work on the record, and there's an interesting rhythmic quirk in verse two.

The choruses are sung by Rabin and Squire and are clearly unchanged from the Cinema version, although Anderson embellishes with a 'see it through' to remind us he's there. The unusual vocal section – with lyrics probably by Anderson, in which he tells us 'I believe in neutrality' – leads into another iteration of the chorus and another guitar motif before the chorus is repeated several times. This is followed by 'sunshine shine on, shine on through', a moment where Rabin's lyrics – looking towards personal positives in a difficult time – and Anderson's (doing the same thing at a time of global uncertainty) dovetail. There's a big guitar solo to finish. It's stirring stuff.

'It Can Happen' (Squire/Anderson/Rabin) (5.29)

Guest musician: Deepak Khazanchi (sitar, tambura)

Chart places: UK: 92, US: 51

Squire wrote this song on piano and Rabin wrote the sitar-style introduction. It's the one song on *90125* that we know about in some detail since the Cinema version is in the public domain on the *Yesyears* box set. Therefore, it's the one track where we can be sure that Anderson's contributions lifted a decent song up a couple of notches. In the Cinema version, Squire sings the verse melody. It's decent enough, but it lacks inspiration. These are replaced by an effects-laden verse sung by Anderson, once again tackling weightier subjects than Squire's more personal lyric. Squire provides the stuttering (but highly effective) backing vocals across some heavily reverbed piano. Squire's bass riff that runs through the intro, with its Eastern effects, is another quirky delight.

Squire's lyrics and melody are retained for the pre-chorus, which is more conventional in tone, with a chugging guitar, although Anderson takes over for the 'It Can Happen' refrain before an Anderson-dominated middle eight leads into the pre-chorus and chorus once again.

The almost unintelligible spoken word section over Rabin's (very good) solo is from *The Importance Of Being Earnest* by Oscar Wilde, and we then go into a section where the refrain is repeated, and Rabin adds some 'la la' vocals. While the first three minutes of the song are full of interest, this is one that actually benefitted from having a minute removed for its single version, which takes out the solo and Oscar Wilde section, good though it is.

British-Indian musician Deepak Khazanchi, best known as part of the Bhangra music group Heera, plays on this track, adding an Eastern flavour, although similar lines are played by Rabin in the earlier version.

'Changes' (Rabin/Anderson/ White) (6.20)

From a song that outlives its welcome slightly to a brilliantly crafted, stone-cold Yes classic. Without a doubt, it is in this author's top ten.

If there's one song that sums up the journey that the music for this album went on, it's this. It began as a fairly straightforward Rabin song, with a personal lyric, written during a period of mild depression for the guitarist as his development deal with Geffen was failing. While the subject of his lyric is general enough to be anyone – friend, lover, family member, for instance – it is most likely to be the Geffen organisation itself, which Rabin felt had turned on him. The song then went into the Cinema machine for arrangement, and at some point, White wrote the percussion introduction. He later heard it in a mall and wondered if he should be getting a personal royalty on it. The progressive section after that part is thrilling, as it morphs into a 4/4 section and the song itself begins, sung by Rabin. 'I'm moving through some changes, I'll never be the same', he sings, before Anderson and Squire take up the chorus, singing Rabin's lyrics. It's tuneful, powerful and moving, allowing Rabin to riff away with passion. In fact, it's the emotion in the song that makes it – and those emotions belong to Rabin.

That said, one of the great pleasures of this album remains the number of times we get to hear Anderson and Squire sing together. Although there are some instances on other albums, it's a unique noise that is heard less often on Yes albums than you'd think – it's far more prevalent when the band play live.

The 'one word from you, one word from me' section is all Anderson. Again, he discusses 'liberty', although here, he's more interested in the effect that love has in bringing about change. One suspects Rabin might not be thinking anything as profound as that, but the two sets of lyrics work nicely together.

The piece ends after a final chorus and a reprise of the complex progressive section, closing side one in triumph. It's thrilling stuff.

'Cinema' (Squire/Rabin/White/Kaye) (2.07)
Fading in on a drum roll and a bass drone, this short piece has the feel of an introduction, and indeed, it was originally planned as the opening section of the legendary 'lost' 20-minute piece 'Time'. Here, it acts as an introduction to the entirely different 'Leave It'. It was recorded at AIR Studios in London, where (despite Squire's lateness) they managed to get a great drum sound. There's a tambourine in the mix that irritates this listener, but aside from that, it's a great piece of work based around a wonderful Rabin guitar melody, aided by a terrific rolling bassline and some triumphant synth. It could almost be 1970s Yes, except for some overdriven feedback howls from Rabin's guitar that place the track squarely in the hard rock era. The piece is also the only one on the album to feature Trevor Horn's voice, the producer adding to the angelic 'ah, ah's towards the end of the piece. It's utterly magnificent and a great showcase for Alan White's virtuosity.

'Leave It' (Rabin/Squire/Horn) (4.13)
Guest Musician: Graham Preskett: violin
Chart places: UK: 56, US: 24
Initially conceived as an *a cappella* number, this song – the catchy second single from the album – was written and recorded by Rabin and Squire, with Rabin writing the melody and Squire the main bass riff, which is played on a variety of instruments. In the end, they decided to add some basic instrumentation – electronic drums, synth, bass and, later in the song, violin and guitar. However, the astonishing overdubbed vocals are the main selling point here, recorded when they couldn't get a drum sound for the song (probably at Sarm East, then). However, once the vocals had been recorded, the engineer accidentally wiped the time code. Rabin then transferred all the parts into a Synclavier and physically played them back into the song. Nevertheless, with the results not as good as they had hoped, they then decided to re-record all the vocals from scratch. To stress – the layered vocals were not enhanced mechanically – they were recorded one at a time from scratch.

Rabin takes the first verse and Anderson (who has no writing credit) the second, singing part of it in harmony with Squire. He also embellishes at several points in the song, firstly with a little cod-scat and right at the end, part-speaking the opening line. Once again, his contributions enhance an already bold but tuneful piece of music.

The song breaks down at 2:40 into a tense instrumental section, with vocals reduced to 'oooo's before electronic percussion crashes, introducing a conventional middle eight sung by Rabin. This is then followed by a return to the jaunty chorus and final embellishments from both lead vocalists.

Despite no input from Anderson whatsoever, the lyrics are somewhat abstract, seemingly warning against the pleasures of the flesh for a band on the road, as spiritual pursuits are favoured over a 'young man's pleasures' via

'Goodbye bad, hello heaven'. Double-syllable words are useful rhythmically when compiling bands of layered vocals, so this may also have been a factor in the lyrical choice here. The song references MacArthur Park – almost certainly not the Jimmy Webb song of the same name, popularised by Richard Harris, Glenn Campbell and Donna Summer – but more a reference to the area in Los Angeles.

The second single after 'Owner', 'Leave It' fared less well, although it did reach number 24 in the US charts. In the UK, it reached a lowly number 56.

Whereas the single version of 'Owner' might need to be sought out on YouTube, the single edit of 'Leave It' is available on the expanded and remastered version of the album, released in 2004. It's a tight, shorter mix with slightly different instrumental effects and toned-down guitars. The expanded version also shows how the song might have sounded in its originally intended *a capella* form, and it's rather effective.

Like 'Owner', 'Leave It' was also given a bold remix, this time 'edited' by engineer Stuart Bruce and Chris Squire. At 9.04 (and played at 33 1/3 rpm), it's a gruelling listen unless you are in a club. It's called the 'Hello, Goodbye' mix for good reason – this refrain (sung by Anderson) and the keyboard chord sequence are pretty much all that's left from the band's version.

'Our Song' (Squire/Rabin/Horn/Kaye) (4.18)

If you are going to put a weak track on an album, as the old adage (that I've just made up) goes, bury it halfway through side two. This was the fate of 'Our Song'. Seemingly the most 'ordinary' song on the album and played least on the *90125* tour, it was worked up during the Cinema rehearsals (thus the credit for all four members), with some late input from Anderson. The good news, however, is that this is by no means filler – it's a little gem.

Beginning with an airy synth motif, bass, guitar and drums break in, in a somewhat off-kilter way, showing a fair degree of playfulness with rhythm and metre as the band throw in bars of 3/4, 4/4 and 2/4 seemingly (to this listener at least) at random. This playfulness continues as the verse starts, sung by Anderson, with further bars of 3/4 and 4/4, held together by some remarkable drumming from Alan White. Only in the lines just before the chorus does the metre resolve to 4/4, and the song takes on a more conventional structure into the chorus. There's a guitar break before the second verse, which shows Rabin's mastery of guitar texture, even in 1983 – this would reach full fruition with *Talk* ten years later. The rhythm part is overdriven; the lead guitar is clean. The keyboard sounds – spacey synth and an airy, synthetic-sounding piano – betray the early 1980s era of the album's recording. Squire's bass is both solid and full of energy and flies free as the introduction is repeated and the song finishes after just over four breathless minutes.

The 'Toledo' referred to in the song is not the town in Spain (sadly) but the city in Ohio, and according to White, this is a reference to a Yes show on the

Going For The One tour at Toledo Sports Arena on 30 July 1977, at which the temperature rose to 126 degrees F. The song also references 'Rule Britannia', although with no real meaning except that the band – at that time – were 100% British! Aside from that, the song seems to be a tribute to the power of music. A noble sentiment.

'City Of Love' (Rabin/Anderson) (4.52)
From a song that was clearly created by the full band through trial and error in the rehearsal room to one that was crafted largely by Rabin alone. However, Anderson's input cannot be overstated. The song really benefits from the vocalist's 'rock' voice, lyrics and vocal melody – one wonders what Rabin's original version sounded like. Hopefully, we'll find out eventually!

Rabin discussed the track with Mike Tiano of *Notes From The Edge* in 2003:

> When we finished the back[ing] track for 'City Of Love', that was a pretty special moment because it was live. There are overdubs, but the essence of the song is live. Everything that was overdubbed on the song was vocal or kind of dressing. When we came into the control room and listened to it, and Trevor Horn turned it up – we did it at the Townhouse – we all went, 'Wow!'

Rabin's echoed 'City Of Love' voice intones over a two-note riff, initially played by the bass and then taken up by heavy guitar and drums. This song vies with 'Real Love' from *Talk* as the band's heaviest. It works because the band are aiming at a sleazy tone and succeeding, although, like 'Owner', it hardly feels like Yes, and there's even a touch of reggae in the second half of the verse. Anderson – not for the first time – harmonises with Squire over a staccato synth. The chorus, when it comes, breaks the tension and sounds unchanged from the Cinema version, with massed vocals from Rabin and Squire and a catchy synth riff. Verse two feels like Anderson had more lyrical input, and in the harmony section, he sings with himself rather than Squire (an interesting moment of arrangement detail). Rabin throws in some vocal variations into the second chorus, and the band throw in a unison, heavy rock section before a brief howl of guitar and verse three, with Anderson singing, 'once bitten twice shy, no woman no cry' – a reference to the Bob Marley song. Marley was a big influence on Anderson, as he exemplified when he wrote about the Jamaican on the song 'The Messenger' from *The Ladder* album in 1999. Another unison heavy rock section leads into Rabin's bold feedback-laden solo and a sudden end.

The tone of the piece and the lyrics – which describe, in lurid detail, a place of prostitution and drug selling – were inspired by an accidental trip to Harlem in New York City when he was asked to try out as keyboard player with Foreigner but went to the wrong address. Rabin got lucky and avoided trouble, but the experience fired his imagination.

The song has featured on every tour by Rabin-era Yes, where it has usually been greatly extended, allowing Rabin lengthy solo time.

'Hearts' (Anderson/Squire/Rabin/White/Kaye) (7.43)
The obvious closer on *90125*, 'Hearts' is the most obviously 'Yessy' song on the album. How ironic, then, that it should remain – like 'Endless Dream' on *Talk* – this author's least favourite track for many years. A view I've now revised, I might add. It is also the song that clearly has the most 'interference' from Anderson, particularly in terms of lyrics, but his influence in the countermelody in the verses can also be felt.

This was another song with elements written by Rabin during the Geffen period and worked up in rehearsal in Cinema. Kaye wrote the delicate keyboard and percussion riff that starts the song, with Rabin's melody on top of that – 'set your heart sail on the river'. Anderson wrote the countermelody: 'hearing, talking, yes, I love you'. Interestingly, a regular Yes lyrical theme raises its head: the concept of life – in this case, a life with one's chosen partner – being a moving river, first discussed in *Close To The Edge*, but here, initially a product of Rabin's imagination rather than Anderson's. The sentiment of the song is also very Yes-like in that its message is relatively simple. Love – as Anderson often tells us – is the answer, and we need to teach this to our children, too (another Anderson lyrical trope). It's clear that apart from the chorus and Rabin's parts of the verse, the lyrics are very much Anderson's. 'Be ready now, be ye circle. Be the central force ye life' – only Anderson would have attempted a lyric like that.

The opening verse is pensive – Anderson begins, followed by Rabin's line, and then they sing in harmony, with Squire joining. White plays a simple beat while Squire's bass doubles the keyboard riff, which repeats throughout this section. A linking instrumental passage heralds the next verse, again sung by Anderson, but with backing vocals now taking on the tone of a Gregorian chant, giving this section something of an ecclesiastical tone. After '... be ready to move', we enter the chorus, Anderson in counterpoint with Rabin and Squire's backing vocals.

A return to the opening lines now introduces a heavy, somewhat conventional (but beautifully played, of course) bluesy guitar solo, Kaye's riff and some powerful drums from White (and just a touch of complexity in the bass part) continuing. For some, this might be a touch too much since, up to now, it's all been very intricate and delicate, but this is a different Yes – one that merges progginess with accessible blues chops. We're back to the chorus, and there would be a case for finishing the song there, but no – we have another section, a thrilling surge of old-school Hammond from Kaye over a heavy rock and synth riff (C and D repeated rhythmically) from Rabin. Anderson, drenched in reverb, now gives us the moment of lyrical doubt – 'who would believe you, wise men do' – and we now have a rocked-up version of the opening riff before a return to the chorus, and a more melodic (but still somewhat shreddy) solo from Rabin. A final coda from Anderson over a simple keyboard backing closes the song and, indeed, the whole album.

For some years, I thought this was the song in which the combination of Anderson's delicacy and extreme romanticism fought head to head with Rabin's hard rock leanings, cancelling each other out. But as the years have gone by and the fandom of Rabin has increased, I've warmed to the contrasts. I still think – had the Rabin that made *Rio* and even *Talk* stepped up to the plate here, as opposed to the one that had just made three heavy rock albums for Chrysalis – he might have handled the guitar textures with more restraint. But 'Hearts' represents a moment in time – it remains a 'showcase' track that has stood the test of time, as well as 'Owner' and 'Changes'.

Contemporary Recordings

As already mentioned in passing, the band – minus Anderson, but with Kaye, of course – recorded some 'work in progress' material at a location called Sunpark Studios, London. It's clear that this is another name for Chris Squire's converted garage studio at New Pipers in Virginia Water, Surrey, since the Squire solo section of *9012Live – The Solos* was also mixed there. Tony Kaye also confirmed to the author that some material was recorded there.

The sessions were engineered by Trevor Rabin and Nigel Luby (who is sadly no longer with us); the latter had been engineering the rehearsal sessions in Islington. Two of these pieces appear on the *Yesyears* box set. However, the date given for these sessions is January 1981, which – unless I've got the timeline very wrong – is impossible. Rabin had just moved to Los Angeles, and Squire and White were just recovering from the end of the *Drama* tour. Indeed, January 1982 is unlikely – so we must be talking about January 1983 (if January is the correct month). These pieces of music are sophisticated, well recorded and sound well-rehearsed. A third piece, 'It's Over', which sounds like it was recorded at the same sessions, appeared on the Rhino reissue of *90125*, released in 2004.

'Make It Easy' (Rabin) (6.11)

Available on the Yesyears box set

Also known in demo form as 'Take It Easy', this was one of the songs Trevor Rabin brought lock, stock and barrel. The introduction is initially played by Rabin and Kaye in unison before Squire (on bass pedals) and White come in, and Rabin plays the main, soaring guitar line so familiar from its place as the live introduction to 'Owner'. Rabin's lead vocals are impassioned but a little strained, as he was sometimes on his solo material. There's a nice synth run from Kaye just before the chorus, which is excellent, if very much in Rabin's solo style.

It's not hard to understand why Trevor Horn might have taken against the song. 'I was hurtin' inside, but you gave me a second chance', sings Rabin – I can feel Horn wincing at that lyric even now. But there's an exuberance to the chorus, particularly, that will have made it a close-run thing.

The song and arrangement feel finished, and the added proggy touches, of which there are several – especially in the somewhat wild last few seconds – feel like the product of many hours in a rehearsal room. The backing vocals are rudimentary but in place, and while the drum sound isn't especially crisp, it's not hard to imagine that the band thought that this was a shoo-in for the album.

'Make It Easy' was also going to be part of 'Time' and would close that long piece, as suggested in one of Rabin's demos on *90124*.

'It Can Happen' (Cinema Version, written by Squire and Rabin) (6.04)
Available on the Yesyears boxed set and the Rhino remaster of 90125
This is the version of the song that was rehearsed by the band and put onto tape before recording. It begins in broadly the same way, if without the bells and whistles that the Horn-produced version would have. The layered backing vocals are by Squire alone (by the sounds of them), and there's initially some fairly basic synth and some jaunty piano from Kaye. The verse – a bluesy melody sung by Squire, with a staccato guitar from Rabin – was dispensed with entirely when Anderson returned, but the 'look up, look down, look out, look around' pre-chorus remains before the catchy chorus, which again remained intact on the finished version. There's a good solo from Rabin, but the song doesn't really go anywhere, despite a few final 'yeah's from Rabin as the song fades out.

'It's Over' (Rabin) (5.41)
Available on the Rhino remaster of 90125
The drum sound confirms that this was most probably recorded in the same sessions as 'Make It Easy'. It begins with a big, Zeppelin-esque riff, followed by a lead guitar fanfare. Rabin again delivers a slightly strained lead vocal, and the lyrics on the verse are – frankly – terrible, although the chorus – with its Queen-style backing vocals and pensive organ arpeggios – is somewhat better. But of the songs from these sessions that have been released, it's probably the least impressive, although there's some mobile bass from Squire at the end. After a big major chord to finish, the piece feels like it might be going off in another direction as it fades. Was this another section of 'Time'?

'Owner Of A Lonely Heart' (Extended Remix)
A staple part of any single release in the 1980s was the 12" version, and this remix was just that. These remixes fell into two camps – either an enhancement and extension of the main song or an impressionistic dance version, with hardly any melodic relationship to its parent track. Sadly, this falls into the latter category, and as such is hard to listen to outside a club setting. A similar remix of 'Leave It' exists, though only on the 12" single of that song.

90125 Live

The 90125 Tour

It was inevitable that the band would tour in support of the album, which involved visiting the sort of venues that Yes had traditionally played at in the 1970s – big arenas in the US, with a similar schedule in Europe, planned for the summer of 1984, with another visit to the US later that summer. But there were a couple more stings in the tail. The early dates of the tour planned for late January 1984 were postponed when Rabin suffered an unfortunate, if faintly comical, accident in a swimming pool, which led to the removal of his spleen. Or at least one of them. It turned out he had four.

Rabin took a few weeks to recuperate, which also meant time off from practice. He told the author in 2023:

> In the meantime, I'd barely played the guitar, and I certainly hadn't played any of the older Yes stuff. I had never really wanted to call the band Yes in the first place, so now I was stuck playing some of the old Yes tunes in what I considered a new band. Chris reassured me, 'You choose what you want to play'. On the plane to Philadelphia for rehearsal, I came up with some ideas. I was concerned that my guitar style was totally different from Steve Howe's, so Chris also said, 'You do it your way. It'll make the band sound like its own thing'. That made me feel warmer, and it made the tour much easier.

But with the band in rehearsals in early 1984 and a draft set list finally chosen, Kaye had to reproduce a lot of the studio sounds of *90125* live. He needed a keyboard rig that could supply that. Enter Casey Young, an award-winning synthesizer player with a growing portfolio of clients and a reputation for creative keyboard rig creation. Tony Kaye is protective of his role at this time and gives a rather more blunt description of Young's role in the band. 'He was my keyboard tech.' He says. It's understandable. Kaye has been the victim of a conspiracy theory over the years – ridiculous, of course – that he was miming throughout the tour and that Young was actually the keyboard player from below the stage. This is ludicrous for a variety of reasons, particularly as Kaye was clearly a better and more experienced player than Young. The American's expertise was in rig design, not in virtuosity. Technology, not technique, as it were.

Secondly, every bit of footage of the tour demonstrates that Kaye is playing, and finally, while extra musicians are often featured onstage (as Billy Sherwood was during the *Talk* tour in 1994), at this time, they often weren't, especially (though far from exclusively) keyboard players in heavy rock bands.

What Young actually played developed over time. Initially, he was mainly triggering vocal enhancements, such as on 'Changes', but when Anderson suggested he acquire a vocoder (a keyboard device that processes vocal lines, as first used by Yes on the *Drama* album), Young (he claims) had parts thrown at him constantly. Anderson sometimes asked him to play new parts with minutes' notice, and he often had to double Rabin's guitar lines, which took some concentration.

The initial leg of the tour took in the US and Canada from February to May 1984, and after a few weeks' break, the band reconvened in Europe for the summer, arriving in the UK in July. A further two-month jaunt around the US and Canada up to October was followed by the first Rock In Rio at the purpose-built Cidade Do Rock in Rio de Janeiro early in 1985. Almost 1.4 million people attended this ten-day festival, which saw Yes, Queen, George Benson, Rod Stewart and AC/DC each headline two nights. After further dates in Uruguay and Argentina, the *90125* tour officially came to an end in February, a year after it had started.

9012 Live Video, DVD And Live Album

9012live (VHS Video, 1985, DVD version 2006)
Atlantic Video/Warner Music UK Ltd.
Recorded at Northlands Coliseum in Edmonton, Alberta, Canada, on 28 and 29 September 1984
Directed by Steven Soderbergh
Produced by Yes and Tony Dimitriades
VHS running time: 87 minutes
Released November 1985 (US), March 1986 (UK)
Tracklisting:
1. 'Cinema', 2. 'Leave It', 3. 'Hold On', 4. 'I've Seen All Good People', 5. 'Changes', 6. 'Make It Easy (Intro)/Owner Of A Lonely Heart', 7. 'It Can Happen', 8. 'City Of Love', 9. 'Starship Trooper'
DVD only: 'Roundabout'

9012Live The Solos

Atco
US release date: 7 November 1985
UK release date: 17 March 1986
Recorded: 24 June 1984, 28 September 1984 at Westfalenhalle (Dortmund, West Germany), Northlands Coliseum (Edmonton, Alberta, Canada)
Produced by Yes
Running time: 34:24
Released November 1985 (US), March 1986 (UK)
Highest chart placings: none
Tracklisting:
1. 'Hold On', 2. 'Si' (Tony Kaye), 3. 'Solly's Beard' (Trevor Rabin), 4. 'Soon' (Jon Anderson), 5. 'Changes', 6. 'Amazing Grace', 7. 'Whitefish' (Chris Squire and Alan White)
2009 CD reissue bonus tracks: 'City Of Love' and 'It Can Happen'

A little more than one hour of a live show in September 1984, filmed in Edmonton, Canada, was released on VHS in 1985 and later on DVD in 2006, with additional backstage footage, called *Access All Areas*. The film was directed by a young Steven Soderbergh, who would go on to fame with his indie debut, *Sex, Lies And Videotape*, in 1989, and a career that also included the 'Ocean' series starring George Clooney. As well as capturing some excellent concert footage, Soderbergh mixed in footage from a short film called *Young Man's Fancy* from 1952 (effectively an infomercial for Edison Electrics), plus an array of dizzying video effects – that have dated very badly indeed – designed by a company called Charlex. Other dated aspects include the stage clothes – very much 'of their time' – and the stage set itself, spartan in the extreme, emphasising the musicians onstage, all semblance of extraneous equipment hidden from view, a feature of Yes shows until the mid-1990s. Split screen is used to very good effect, however, allowing the viewer access to multiple views, an aspect which has worn rather better.

A 2006 DVD contains an additional version of 'Roundabout', some backstage band footage and a director's cut version that cuts out some – but not all – of the added video footage.

Various bootlegs exist of the entire shows, of course, and some TV footage was shot on video (and so feels quite different, as well as presenting the audio in a slightly rawer form) in Dortmund, Germany, during the European leg in June. The band are in similar stage clothes, except Rabin, who is sporting a striking red jacket.

To accompany the 1985 video was a live album: *9012live The Solos*. While it clearly made sense to release this from a marketing perspective to accompany the video, this one stands out as something of a folly. Although two live tracks are featured – 'Hold On' and 'Changes', from the soundtrack to the video – while a 2009 reissue also adds 'City Of Love' and 'It Can Happen', the rest of the album is very much 'play it once' fodder, containing as it does the solo spots from each of the artists. It's well done, but hardly essential listening. Kaye's solo 'Si' contains some powerful church organ and a snippet of Bach's 'Toccata', while Rabin's 'Solly's Beard', accompanied by Kaye, is flashy but doesn't come across well on record. Anderson gives us 'Soon' from *Relayer*, again with Kaye accompanying, a well-received exercise in nostalgia rather than something with much merit as a listen. The rest of the album (11 minutes, if we're counting) is given over to Squire and White, firstly with the bassist's eardrum-bursting bass pedal rendition of 'Amazing Grace', which he'd also played on the *Drama* tour. They then launch into 'Whitefish', which starts with 'The Fish', before instrumental renditions of 'Tempus Fugit' from *Drama* and 'Sound Chaser' from *Relayer*.

What *9012live The Solos* does do, however, is emphasise the sheer number of people – many of them new members of the team – that went into the creation of such a massive tour. It's notable that South African Paul DeVilliers was the live sound engineer, and the lighting engineer was Merle McLain, so no roles for Nigel Luby and Michael Tait, both of whom had been crucial parts of the Yes team for over ten years.

Page 30 SOUNDS November 26, 1983

EDDIE

ALAN

"THERE IS a disco mix! I believe that it's valid for us to go into these avenues. But I wouldn't say the single itself is actually a disco record, even though they did play it at the Camden Palace last week!" — Chris Squire.

CAN YOU believe it? A sussy, scorching single from the maestros that sculptured 'Close To The Edge', 'Tales From Topographic Oceans' and 'Going For The One'.

Make no mistake, Yes are back with a crash and a bang or two! Crashing back into action with 'Owner Of A Lonely Heart', a dynamic ditty with cacophonic, diametric instrumental bangs and blasts laced with infectious melodies and a breakneck squealer of a lead break.

Jon Anderson is pleased. "Love lost, love won, or it could be happening ... someone looking for love. These are supposed to be the three main options for a hit record, aren't they? Which one's 'Owner Of A Lonely Heart' then? *I don't know!*"

It's a curious re-entry into the arena for the imperial imp and the merry Yes-men. Instant mass appeal guaranteed by a careful balancing of opening HM chordery, a neat beat *for the* feet, and an irresistable hookline. Anderson thinks that essentially it's not *really* that far removed from the olden structured epics, rather systematically streamlined.

"I actually always wrote short songs, I used to like piecing them together with songs by Steve (Howe, as if you need reminding). Because I always felt there was more substance to a seven minute song than a three-minuter. To me, in some ways, that was the wrong way of thinking because you should be able to condense as well as expand. I started to think about expansion simply as a defence mechanism of not being able to make hit singles with the 'progressive' music we made in the early days.

"For instance, I think 'And You And I' was just a little song, but we developed it into a meaningful structure of music! It was only four chords!"

Careful Jon, you might destroy some people's illusions!

"True, but music *is* an illusion in a lot of ways."

Few folks should know better. Anderson's celebrating two decades in 'da biz' this year. Twelve of those years he and Squire devoted to building Yes into the immense supergroup they're remembered as: church organs and lush vocal harmonies, stunning stageshows and surreal Roger Dean sleeves, magnificent musicianship on monumental masterpieces, such were the hallmarks, the mention of which usually draws reactions of nostalgia or nausea.

CHRIS SQUIRE's Rolls-Royce Silver Cloud, sitting outside the Knightsbridge Hilton where in turn new guitarist Trevor Rabin and he gave their new Yes stories, is just one souvenir of that bygone era of rock opulence.

(The Anderson interview was conducted a couple of days later in a hired Chelsea mansion, while Alan White was off chasing the eagle that escaped while filming the 'Lonely Heart' video, eventually it was captured on Tower Bridge after a dramatic cross-London dash!)

Jon Anderson and Rick Wakeman were, of course, replaced in Yes by Buggles Trevor Horn and Geoff Downes in 1980, an ambitious merging that gave the band's lease of life a ten-month extension.

But Hammersmith Odeon in December of that year saw the last time Yes trod the boards, and it seemed that the curtain had finally come down on one of Britain's all-time Mega-groups.

Of course Steve Howe, together with ex-Yes manager Brian Lane, has since found further multi-platinum satisfaction in Asia, and it never seemed probable that Yes might one day reform without him. But they have! It was not, however, an instant decision, Squire swears.

Dateline London, early 1982: "Since the last format of Yes split up Alan and I had been doing some things together, the 'Run With The Fox' single at Christmas in 1981. Then we thought it would be more constructive to put a band together, that wasn't necessarily going to be anything to do with Yes."

Dateline Los Angeles, early 1982: South African guitarist (and not many people know this, a qualified classical conductor too!) Trevor Rabin, with a string of albums behind him — first with Rabbit, homeland heroes, then solo — is about to sign his latest project to RCA shortly after rejecting a "cut and dried" proposition to join a forming British-based supergroup, Asia!

"Then there was this call from Chris, thru the record company. Mutt Lange had recommended me so Chris said come over and let's play. Alan, Chris and I went to Chris's studio and mucked around, and it *felt* good. So I went back to LA while we were deciding what to do, and Chris came up with the idea of bringing Tony Kaye in."

Kaye, for those uninitiated, was the original Hammond handler in Yes from 1968 to 1971. However, he never made the reformed Yes, being nudged out last winter soon after recording started with Trevor Horn at the helm, reportedly (officially) because he didn't fancy touring.

"Oh ... oh ... sorry ... Tony didn't wanna tour," jests Rabin. "Hey, I'm gonna tell you the the truth! Tony and Trevor didn't seem to get on. Also Tony's not very familiar with the new gear. He's a great Hammond player, but as far as the new, computerised keyboards go he's not really into that."

So Rabin doubled on synthesiser for the sessions, and by late July this year, after months in and out of London and Home Counties studios the backing tracks were complete. Seemingly self-indulgent, perhaps, but Rabin promises that "we went in and we *worked*."

Squire picks up the tale. "We got to that point, the ideas in most of the songs were fully written, there were a few blank spaces. The original intention was for Trevor and I to do vocals. But I just ... I can't say it wasn't always possibly in the back of my mind to reform Yes, but it wasn't the plan. The reason why we didn't carry on as it was, was I just saw it could be much, much better."

Enter Jon Anderson, a minute gent whose native Lancashire lingo is tinted by years of US touring, and whose conversation is illuminated by plenty of pensiveness.

"Chris gave us a call, asked if I'd like to hear some of the music he'd been working on, because they felt they were going somewhere but it wasn't really taking off. I hadn't seen Chris since I left, so it was nice for him to ring up and chat anyway. So we popped down the local pub, he played me a tape, and it just excited me, the overall prospect of working on that music.

"But I said to Chris at that first meeting, if I start singing on top of this, it's gonna sound like Yes. Because obviously the dominant rhythm section and vocals were very complementary to the idea of what Yes was all about. The top line voice and Chris's style of bass hopefully always complement each other, and the rest is adding to the style."

So, although Eddie Jobson completed the line-up only weeks before these here chinwags, there's no prizes for guessing that Anderson's recruitment was when the project *became* Yes.

Squire: "I still felt that it didn't necessarily *have* to be. But the band was to be called Cinema, and we actually started to have problems using that name. As soon as it was announced in *The Standard* and in a couple of places in America we suddenly got all these letters — 'We're from Iowa and we're called Cinema.'"

Queueing to sue?

"That's right. And I thought it was so funny that there was already four of them and they hadn't bothered to sue each

Above: Part of an interview from *Sounds* magazine in November 1983, clearly showing that Eddie Jobson was considered a full time member. For a while at least. (*David Watkinson Collection*)

Big Generator (1987)

Personnel:
Jon Anderson: vocals
Chris Squire: bass, vocals
Trevor Rabin: guitar, keyboards, vocals, string arrangements
Alan White: drums, percussion, vocals
Tony Kaye: Hammond organ and piano
James Zavala: horns on 'Almost Like Love', harmonica on 'Love Will Find A Way'
Lee R. Thornburg: horns on 'Almost Like Love'
Nick Lane: horns on 'Almost Like Love'
Greg Smith: horns on 'Almost Like Love'
Recorded at Lark Studios, Italy; Sarm and Air studios, London, and Southcombe, Westlake and Sunset Sound studios, Los Angeles, between 1985 and 1987.
Produced by Yes, Trevor Horn, Trevor Rabin, Paul De Villiers
Released: September 1987
Highest chart positions: UK: 17, US: 15
Running time: 43:48

Ending the tour at the start of 1985, what Yes should have done was produce a new album quickly, and have it out in early 1986 at the latest. What they actually did was lurch from studio to studio, getting very little done and spending huge amounts of money. The band recorded in Italy, to begin with. This was partially for tax reasons and partially because Rabin wanted the band to gel as a unit, with Trevor Horn again producing. Anderson's presence was not needed for the first few weeks, and when he got to Italy, he found partying and very little work. When these sessions proved unfruitful, they switched to Sarm East and West in London, at which point Trevor Horn jumped ship, and the album was finished in Los Angeles with Rabin and Paul DeVilliers producing.

There seem to have been a few power struggles, initially between Rabin and Horn, and later between Rabin and Anderson, over songwriting direction. In short, Yes went through the same sort of issues that many rock bands experienced in the 1980s. There was too much money available, and the band got locked into its own ego bubble – unable to see the bigger picture. After a tour promoting this album that visited the US and Japan but not Europe, Anderson decided to move on again. Kaye also had his issues, and once again is probably absent from most of the album. Early on, he clashed with Horn again, but remained in the band this time.

In truth, you can hear the indecision in the final product. While most of the material is decent, the album's soullessness creates a barrier between the listener and the band. Ironically, the shorter, more modern-sounding material on side one (of the vinyl) is the more impressive. In contrast, the two longer tracks on side two – 'I'm Running' and 'Final Eyes' – although a little more progressive in spirit, lack intimacy. The fact that there are three songs on the album with 'love' in the title shows what the band were aiming at. After the immediacy of *90125, Big Generator* feels hugely overproduced with its layered backing vocals – with Squire's usually distinctive vocals often buried – and over-busy instrumentation.

The Alternative Generator, a bootleg CD which we'll look at in slightly more detail at the end of this chapter, may give an unbalanced perspective, so needs treating with kid gloves. But it does suggest that Rabin's hands were on the tiller from the word go, and that he was almost as dominant as he had been on *90125*. Anderson's influence, if there was any at all, was with a further sprinkling of fairy dust. Sadly, this time the dust didn't settle.

'The Rhythm Of Love' (Kaye, Rabin, Anderson, Squire)
The first track of any album often sets the tone of what is to follow, and it does here. It is a big, reverb-heavy rocker, albeit with some subtle touches in the middle eight. A minor hit as a single in the US, reaching number 40, it has become the most-played song from the album in the live set over the years. The band even persuaded Howe to do a very creditable job playing it on the 2004 *World* tour, and it represented the album when Anderson, Rabin and Wakeman performed it on their 2017 and 2018 live dates. In the context of this 'new' version of Yes, it is very good indeed, although the 'love' it talks about here is 'carnal' rather than 'brotherly'. It was also played live on the *Big Generator* tour as the set opener.

'Big Generator' (Rabin, Kaye, Anderson, Squire, White)
So to the title track, which mixes the orchestral 'stabs' from 'Owner' with the heaviest riffs yet heard on a Yes album (even if 'City Of Love' remains the heaviest track overall). It balances a tense verse sung by Anderson with a chorus that contrasts high- and low-register vocals, dominated by Rabin. This is impressive stuff, the relative simplicity of the song contrasting with some interesting production techniques and some inventive, King Crimson-style guitar. The 'flying out the soft machine' section sounds like Godley and Creme, particularly some of the vocal techniques used on the *L* and *Freeze Frame* albums. It was played live on the *Big Generator* tour.

'Shoot High, Aim Low' (White, Kaye, Rabin, Anderson, Squire)
Languid and quietly inventive, 'Shoot High, Aim Low' has some lovely acoustic guitar quite low in the mix, and – aside from the more obvious 'Changes' – has the best use of Anderson and Rabin sharing lead vocal duties.

White's drum part was recorded in Italy, using the natural reverb available in the house they were staying in. The song takes its time to develop, with deftly-planted keyboards sweeping in and out of the mix. If the criticism that the album is 'over-produced' can be levelled at it, then this song is the worst offender, yet it works here. Unusual and powerful, it is probably the highlight of the album. It was played live on the *Big Generator* tour.

'Almost Like Love' (Kaye, Rabin, Anderson, Squire)
I've always had a sneaking liking for this somewhat unsung track. It certainly rubbed a lot of Yes fans up the wrong way with its Motown-style drum pattern and – gasp – a horn section, playing the song's main riff. While it couldn't be any more different from the Yes of *Close To The Edge,* it has an exuberance of its own. Anderson delivers one of his part-scat/part-raps, and there's some great Hammond from Kaye and a speedy guitar solo from Rabin. It's hardly a classic, but as an old-fashioned up-tempo closer to side one of the vinyl version, it's rather tasty. The song was played as the set opener on the 1987 leg of the *Big Generator* tour but was dropped in favour of 'Rhythm Of Love' in 1988.

'Love Will Find A Way' (Rabin)
A string quartet introduces this Rabin pop/rock song, originally written for Stevie Nicks. It has an infectious sing-along quality, and it is not hard to see it as a big hit for Nicks. For Yes, it was a minor one, reaching number 30 in the US and number 73 in the UK. While Rabin is the lead vocalist, Anderson and Squire both make good contributions, and there are short solos for Kaye and James Zavala, who plays harmonica (not Squire, as some listeners assume!). It was played live on the *Big Generator* tour.

'Final Eyes' (Rabin, Kaye, Anderson, Squire)
This longer piece, sung by Anderson – with help on some lines from Rabin – feels like an attempt to recapture the magic of the 1970s version of the band. Rabin's guitar actually sounds like Steve Howe until he cranks up the overdrive halfway through, and there are some nostalgic Hammond whirls from Kaye. That said, I find the song unconvincing, perhaps a little too sweet and sentimental in both melody and lyric to feel like 'old' Yes. There are three songs with 'love' in the title on the album, and while 'Final Eyes' isn't one of them, it is the most syrupy of the lot.

The Alternative Generator (see below) version is a very different beast, suggesting that Rabin reworked this song completely during the edit in California. There's a Rabin-sung verse that isn't bad, with Anderson singing the 'you were there when I needed someone' section. Many of the melodic elements and Rabin's fairly conventional break-up-song lyrics remain. The final version is probably better, but structurally feels like an extended ballad.

'I'm Running' (Rabin, Squire, Anderson, Kaye, White)
Rather better, but still not quite up there with the band's best work, is 'I'm Running'. Squire's terrific bass riff – with treble turned up to the max – introduces the piece, a difficult opening that leads into the main verse, with its chanted chorus. This is by far the most progressive piece on the album, albeit awash with 1980s production techniques, with piano – probably played by Rabin in effect-laden form – and Kaye's organ heavily featured. This is a

piece worthy of further examination, and it would certainly be interesting if Rabin-orientated lineups at least had a stab at playing this track live in the future.

The lyrics feel like they were written by Rabin with tweaks by Anderson, *90125*-style.

While broadly following the same structure, the *Alternative Generator* version sounds a little basic and stripped back, though Anderson's vocals are terrific. It may be the same lead vocal as the completed version, yet without the production sheen it has more bite.

'Holy Lamb (Song For Harmonic Convergence)' (Anderson)
The sort of Anderson piece that he loves to close albums with, this song is throwaway stuff, and belongs on a solo record rather than a Yes album. Here, it feels underdeveloped and something of an afterthought, perhaps an attempt to keep Anderson happy on an album he felt he had not contributed enough to. It didn't work, and nor does the track. It was, however, played live on the *Big Generator* tour.

The song has one unusual admirer. Yes keyboardist in the new millennium, Oliver Wakeman, has always loved the song and considered playing it at solo shows, although at the time of writing he has yet to do so.

Related Tracks
There are no related songs from this era, though the 2009 reissue includes various contemporary remixes of 'Love Will Find A Way' and 'The Rhythm Of Love'.

The Alternative Generator
Sonic Boom Records
Released: 2024
It's not entirely clear whether this professional-looking release is a bootleg, so we won't dwell on it for too long, but it offers alternative takes, working versions and demos from the album sessions. These are fairly low-fi versions, so they were most likely taken from a secondary source.

It's not quite clear at what stage many of these versions were created, but (for instance) 'Love Will Find A Way' is clearly a Rabin-sung demo, as it's intact but missing Anderson, the string quartet and the harmonica part. The version of 'The Rhythm Of Love' is interesting in that vocally it has Rabin mimicking Anderson as a guide vocal. 'Holy Lamb' is an ambient instrumental that has the same chord structure but bears no other relation to the final song, and so might have been brought along by Anderson, as he has the only writing credit on the final version.

Both versions of the title track give few further clues to the song's development, although the two versions of 'Shoot High Aim Low' are interesting signposts to the completed mixes.

Anderson, Bruford, Wakeman, Howe (1989)

Personnel:
Jon Anderson: vocals
Steve Howe: guitars
Rick Wakeman: keyboards
Bill Bruford: electronic and acoustic drums
Tony Levin: bass, stick, vocals
Matt Clifford: keyboards, programming, orchestration, vocals
Milton McDonald: rhythm guitar
Backing vocals: The Oxford Circus Singers – Deborah Anderson, Tessa Niles, Carol Kenyon, Francis Dunnery
JMC Singers: Jon Anderson, Matt Clifford, Chris Kimsey
Emerald Community Singers, Montserrat
Produced at Air Studios, Montserrat, and Air Studios, London, by Chris Kimsey and Jon Anderson. Recorded 1988 and early 1989
Pre-production recording at Studio La Frette, Paris
Released: 20 June 1989
Highest chart places: UK: 14, US: 30
Running time: 59:05

Yes, I know. This is not a Yes album, and as a result, not part of the 'catalogue'. However, so crucial is it to the fate of the band over the next few years of its turbulent existence that I have taken a little poetic licence – for one album only in this volume, although I'll be doing something similar in the next volume – and included it. Some people will consider this an 'honorary' Yes album anyway, as I do. Others will be vehemently opposed – many Yes fans love to be vehemently opposed to things – but I hope they will, at least, understand my logic, and bear with me.

Yes albums have been created in many ways. Although most often collaborative, if not always democratic, sometimes the impetus has come from one or a group of musicians, with others falling in line; *Open Your Eyes* would be a good example. In the case of *Anderson, Bruford, Wakeman, Howe,* the impetus came from a frustrated Jon Anderson, who had suffered several years as a bit-part player in his own movie. He had recorded a solo album, *In The City Of Angels,* released in the spring of 1988, which had failed to trouble any charts, despite its commercial leanings. With the support of his wife, Jennifer, who felt that it was time for 1970s-style Yes to make a return, he decided that he wanted a band, and he knew some musicians that might be interested...

Anderson had not played with Steve Howe for ten years. He had not played with Bruford since 1972, but Howe had used Bruford as a session player on a few occasions. Anderson had also become firm friends with Wakeman, but they hadn't played together since his appearance on Wakeman's 1981 solo album *1984*. In this case, all were recruited separately, and they all supplied some material, particularly Howe.

He then formed a temporary band based around keyboard player Matt Clifford and guitarist Milton McDonald to create demos in a studio in Paris. Then Wakeman and Bruford joined Anderson at George Martin's Air Studios in Montserrat to record the album. Howe chose not to go, recording his guitars on his own in London. Initially, Anderson had hoped that Squire would join the project at some point, but with Bruford preferring not to work with him, the drummer suggested his former King Crimson cohort Tony Levin, who did a sterling job. Experienced producer Chris Kimsey, best known to progressive rock fans for his work with Marillion, was brought in by new record company Arista, nervous about allowing Anderson too much freedom.

The resulting album was well received and sold well for Arista, certified gold in the US. Was this old-style Yes? Had the band achieved what it wanted? Yes and no. There are aspects of the album that really work; it certainly has energy and commitment from all the players. There are hints of what the Bruford-era band might have sounded like had it stayed together beyond 1972, and also what the *Tormato* lineup might have produced had it fought its way past its differences. Bruford's electronic drums, in particular, create a tone unlike anything ever heard before on a Yes project, even if those sounds have dated badly. Furthermore, I really miss the intricacy of Bruford's acoustic playing; on this album, his textures are largely in the sounds he creates, not in his actual playing technique.

Also somewhat dated are some of Wakeman's keyboard patches, although one of the delights of the album is the huge amount of piano on it. Yet I can never quite escape the feeling that what I am listening to is an enhanced Jon Anderson solo album. Musically, it goes in places that, I suspect, Squire would never have allowed, and as a result, feels like an album with various aspects of the Yes sound, rather than an album that is awash with it. Nonetheless, as a possible Yes in an alternative universe, it is as valid as any of the 'fringe' albums, like *Fly From Here* or even *Big Generator*.

'Themes (Sound/Second Attention/Soul Warrior)' (Anderson, Bruford, Wakeman, Howe)

This is a strong start; Wakeman's introduction, played on piano and synthesizer, is very impressive, although as soon as Bruford's electronic drums enter, we know we are in the 1980s. It's a powerful opening, given something of a Yes vibe with Howe's lead work and Wakeman's jaunty synthesizer soloing. The 'Soul Warrior' section, again, suggests a version of Yes that is absorbing new styles and sounds. No Yes album ever sounded quite like this. Overall, 'Themes' is an excellent beginning, and was included in the subsequent tour.

'Fist Of Fire' (Anderson, Bruford, Wakeman, Howe)

The momentum is maintained by this exuberant short piece. Like 'Themes', Anderson's vocal is percussive, even aggressive, and Bruford's electronic percussion really works here. However, the star is Wakeman, swamping the track with thrilling Minimoog solos over a rich poly-synthesizer backing, while Howe also embellishes impressively. It is perfection in 3.32 minutes. An alternative mix of the track, featuring much more guitar, was included on the *In A Word* boxed set. In truth, I prefer the original. Howe, recording on his own, played a lot more guitars than are heard on the final mix of the album, and was (understandably, in a sense) somewhat aggrieved to find a fair amount of what he recorded on the cutting room floor. However, the restored guitars in the alternative version are just too intrusive to be effective.

'Brother Of Mine (The Big Dream/Nothing Can Come Between Us/Long Lost Brother Of Mine)' (Anderson, Bruford, Wakeman, Howe, Geoff Downes)
Despite being the longest piece on the album, I have never been particularly impressed by this track, which feels like three decent, but non-essential songs strung together. 'The Big Dream' and 'Nothing Can Come Between Us' sections definitely have that 'Anderson solo track' feel, although Howe and Wakeman's contributions are impressive, the latter on (digital-sounding) piano. The final section, mainly written by Howe with Geoff Downes, is catchy and, again, Howe and Wakeman make excellent contributions without getting in each other's way. However, except for the final few bars, the instrumentation is embellishment rather than a major part of the piece, and the songs dominate rather than the instrumental sections, for better or worse. Released as a single in the UK, a very short and a longer edit of the track can be found on disc two of the 2014 Esoteric reissue. The piece was played live on the subsequent tour, and a glossy promotional video was recorded for it.

'Birthright' (Anderson, Bruford, Wakeman, Howe, Max Bacon)
Howe's classical guitar comes into its own on this superb track, co-written with his GTR band member Max Bacon, a project that Howe had begun with former Genesis guitarist Steve Hackett a few years before. The lyrics are about the murderous nuclear testing by the British in Woomera, Australia. This is a fantastically atmospheric piece of music, which also makes the best of Wakeman's keyboard parts toward the end of the song, propelled by Bruford's tribal drumming. At just over six minutes, it is the perfect length to tell its story. Again, this was played live on the subsequent tour, and proved something of a show-stopper.

'The Meeting' (Anderson, Bruford, Wakeman, Howe)
Despite the writing credit, this lovely piano and vocal piece has 'Anderson and Wakeman' written all over it. It features one of Wakeman's prettier piano pieces and a typical Anderson melody. It is the only piece from the album that has had any sort of life beyond the life of the band, played as it was as part of the acoustic set on the 2004 Yes *World* tour, and deservedly so, as it's lovely.

'Quartet (I Wanna Learn/She Gives Me Love/Who Was The First/ I'm Alive)' (Anderson, Bruford, Wakeman, Howe, Ben Dowling)
It would be wrong to suggest that the album goes off the rails at this point, but the next two pieces are wafer-thin. Both 'Quartet' and 'Teakbois' are perfectly pleasant but so dominated by somewhat cloying Anderson-penned songs that they waste the musicians playing them. Howe's guitar beginning 'Quartet' is beautiful and Wakeman plays some lovely trumpet-style synthesizer, but this feels more like a Jon and Vangelis track without the invention to the arrangement that Vangelis might bring. The piece also has a false ending before the 'I'm Alive' section, making it feel like a separate track entirely. Overall, 'Quartet' is pleasant enough, but is a rather odd and unsatisfying listen.

'Teakbois' (Anderson, Bruford, Wakeman, Howe)
Something of a 'marmite' track – you either love it or hate it – this piece, clearly inspired by the band's Montserrat location, would never have made it to a Yes album. It's exuberant and fun, and Wakeman is clearly enjoying himself, peeling off various West Indian-inspired solos. I rather like it, I have to admit, and the song should really not be taken too seriously – it's very light-hearted but, again, wafer-thin. The massed vocalists later in the song foreshadow the next track by singing a snatch of the main theme.

'Order Of The Universe (Order Theme/Rock Gives Courage/It's So Hard To Grow/The Order Of The Universe)' (Anderson, Bruford, Wakeman, Howe, Rhett Lawrence)
And so to the big finish. This is a very impressive piece, full of grandeur and, after the lightness of the two tracks before it, it rocks pretty hard, too. The theme – played by Wakeman on synthesizer – is powerful, but Howe's spine-tingling guitar makes the track, before Anderson's rock vocal on 'Rock Gives Courage'. This is somewhat obvious stuff, but we'll allow the band a little rock 'n' roll posturing – it was the 1980s, after all. If anything, 'It's So Hard To Grow' rocks even harder, before the choral 'Order Of The Universe' hook starts to invade the track. There is some great soloing by Howe – criminally low in the mix – a brief, somewhat dated percussion break, then a reprisal of the theme, and the track ends with a flurry of percussion. This piece was, understandably, a centrepiece of the live set on the subsequent tour. 'Rock Gives Courage' was written by Anderson with Rhett Lawrence, presumably during the writing sessions for *In The City Of Angels*, Anderson's 1988 solo album.

'Let's Pretend' (Anderson, Bruford, Wakeman, Howe, Vangelis)
This lovely closing piece is dominated by Howe's classical guitar and a simple, heartfelt vocal from Anderson, with just a touch of synthesizer from Wakeman. It was a result of Anderson's writing sessions with Vangelis the year before, and it's a charming end to the album.

Related Tracks

'Vultures In The City' (Anderson, Bruford, Wakeman, Howe)

A rather slight but atmospheric song, with some nice slide guitar from Howe. It was released as the B-side to 'Brother Of Mine'.

Anderson, Wakeman, Bruford, Howe Live

An Evening OF Yes Music Plus (1993 CD, re-released in 2006, DVD 1997)

Personnel:
Jon Anderson: lead vocals
Bill Bruford: drums, percussion
Rick Wakeman: keyboards
Steve Howe: guitar, backing vocals
Jeff Berlin: bass
Julian Colbeck: additional keyboards, backing vocals
Milton McDonald: rhythm guitar, backing vocals
Recorded 9 September 1989 at Shoreline Amphitheatre
Released December 1993, reissued 2006
No chart placings
Tracklisting:
1. 'The Young Person's Guide To The Orchestra', 2. 'Time And A Word/Owner Of A Lonely Heart/Teakbois/Time And A Word', 3. 'Clap/Mood For A Day', 4. 'Gone But Not Forgotten/Catherine Parr/Merlin The Magician' 5. 'Long Distance Runaround/Bill Bruford Solo', 6. 'Birthright', 7. 'And You And I', 8. 'I've Seen All Good People', 9. 'Close To The Edge', 10. 'Themes', 11. 'Brother Of Mine', 12. 'The Meeting' (DVD Only), 13. 'Heart Of The Sunrise', 14. 'Order Of The Universe', 15. 'Roundabout', 16. 'Starship Trooper'

The project really became a 'band' on the long world tour of 1989, which saw them mixing up material from the album with Bruford-era Yes classics. Again, these concerts felt different, tonally, from the standard Yes shows, with a different structure, especially each band member introducing himself with a solo spot at the start of each show. The live renditions of, for instance, 'Close To The Edge' are full of precision, commitment and power. Seemingly with good album sales and a massively successful tour, against the run of fashion, the future was rosy, and the band would continue as a more collaborative venture. Or would it?

Union (1990)

Personnel:
Jon Anderson: vocals
Chris Squire: bass, vocals
Steve Howe: guitars, vocals
Trevor Rabin: guitars, keyboards, vocals
Tony Kaye: keyboards
Rick Wakeman: keyboards
Alan White: drums, percussion
Bill Bruford: electronic and acoustic drums, percussion
Tony Levin: bass
Jimmy Haun: guitar
Billy Sherwood: vocals and other instruments (uncredited)
Recorded between 1989 and 1991, in various locations
Produced by Jonathan Elias, Steve Howe, Mark Mancina, Eddie Offord, Billy Sherwood
Associate producer: Jon Anderson
Released: 20 April 1991
Highest chart places: UK: 7, US: 15
Running time: 65:23 (standard international CD)

If ever there was an album in the Yes catalogue that typifies the continual infighting and management difficulties over the years, it is the *Union* album. This now seems like an ironic title. In 1990, it was considered appropriate. But that was gaslighting, really.

Anderson, Bruford, Wakeman, Howe, having come off the road, were due to start work on a new album while Yes still technically existed as the remains of the band that had recorded *Big Generator*. Once again, Jon Anderson seems to have been the bridge between the two camps, and with Arista (the ABWH label) after a hit, it seemed that Trevor Rabin's golden pen might be able to provide that. From that, a sort of artificial amalgamation of the two bands seemed to have been worked out, with Anderson singing on the four tracks recorded by the Rabin, Squire, White and Kaye version, and Chris Squire adding vocals to a few of the ABWH tracks.

In a revealing interview with Yes commentator Henry Potts, Jonathan Elias, the producer of the ABWH tracks, paints a picture of a band with almost no material, piecing an album together as the age-old antagonisms began to emerge, mainly between Anderson and Howe and Howe and Wakeman. He describes Anderson and Howe refusing to be in the studio together and Wakeman and Howe refusing to listen to each other's parts, leading to arrangement issues as had been the case on *Tormato*. In the end, Anderson took control of the situation and a host of session players were used – mainly for keyboard parts, but also Jimmy Haun to play some of Steve Howe's guitar lines. These decisions were not well received by either senior musician, as you can imagine.

Union is not the worst album in the Yes catalogue. It actually has some excellent tracks. However, it has no cohesion as a record and many of the ABWH tracks feel underdeveloped. Despite that, it's much too long. With the addition of the rather good 'Give And Take' on the European CD edition, the album comes in at almost 70 minutes, and at least five of the ABWH tracks could have been lost without making the finished product any weaker. It's all a bit of a mess, but when it's good, it's very good.

The main problem is that, after a fairly strong start, the album peters out, with no climactic track to lift the heart. The final few pieces of music may just be the least listened to in Yes history.

On the back of ABWH's success and with some not-inconsiderable buzz around the reunion of all eight musicians, the album did quite well commercially, reaching the UK top ten, but with some poor reviews, the success was not sustained. The subsequent tour, however, was a considerable success, with the eight-piece band playing arenas in the round, as it had in 1978-1979. Wakeman, in particular, really enjoyed it, striking up an unlikely lifelong friendship with the softly spoken Rabin, and while there was some tension between Rabin and Howe, the contrast between White (playing acoustic drums) and Bruford (inventive on his electronic kit) also worked well.

'I Would Have Waited Forever' (Anderson, Howe, Jonathan Elias)
Production: Jonathan Elias
Additional vocals: Chris Squire
This is a strong opening, setting out the 'tone' of the tracks recorded by the ABWH faction. It's hard-ish rock with some progressive and pop twists. Indeed, of all the Yes albums, it is ironic that this is the one that sounds most like Asia. Howe (presumably) delivers a catchy riff and Squire's backing vocals are really effective, although the rhythm guitar sounds like it might be Jimmy Haun. To begin the track with Anderson's catchy vocal hook is also a minor masterstroke. It packs a lot into six and a half minutes and, frustratingly, seems to be going somewhere interesting just as it fades out. Nonetheless, it is a decent start.

'Shock To The System' (Anderson, Howe, Elias)
Production: Jonathan Elias
The momentum continues with another strong track, this time a slice of hard rock with more strong work from Howe (and possibly Haun), and another big riff providing the backbone, even if Anderson's vocal melody betrays a softer edge. It was played by the band early in the set on the Union tour, particularly as it is well suited to the style of both guitarists.

'Masquerade' (Howe)
Production: Steve Howe
There's a history, perhaps even a tradition, of Howe solo pieces on Yes albums, of course, so there's no shame in this track at all, particularly as it's a

lovely piece; one of Howe's finest. It was nominated for a Grammy Award, and deservedly so. However, what it's doing, sequenced third on a full-band album, is another matter. A rather odd decision, but a lovely track.

'Lift Me Up' (Rabin, Squire)
Production: Trevor Rabin
Programming: Mark Mancina
We now switch to the Rabin/Squire version of the band, with this strong offering from Rabin and a song that had originally been offered to the ABWH version of the group, an idea that was abandoned as soon as the 'Union' idea was cooked up. It does demonstrate the contrived nature of some of the recording, however, with Anderson singing the first verse and then becoming buried in the backing vocal arrangement (if he is present at all), with Rabin taking over lead vocals thereafter. In terms of structure, it is fairly typical of Rabin's writing: a catchy pop song encased in a more progressive instrumental framework. The song was predictably released as a single, reaching number 86 in the US, but spending six weeks at number one in the rock chart. As well as being played on the *Union* tour and the *Talk* tour, it was revived for the *Yes – Featuring Anderson, Rabin, Wakeman* tours in 2016 to 2018, giving it a longer life than most pieces from the album.

'Without Hope You Cannot Start The Day' (Anderson, Elias)
Production: Jonathan Elias
Guest vocals: Chris Squire
This maintains the tone of the previous ABWH tracks – a rather decent, gentle opening giving way to something messier and less convincing. Howe (assuming it's him) is impressive, Squire's vocals are again nicely integrated and – for the first time on the album – Wakeman can (probably) be heard, albeit low in the mix. Again it fades out just when it seems to be going somewhere, but overall the track feels cobbled together and might have been better off discarded.

'Saving My Heart' (Rabin)
Production: Trevor Rabin
This slice of Rabin-penned pop and cod-reggae is lightweight in the extreme, but at least holds together as a coherent song, making a better job of integrating Anderson into the mix. To be honest, though, as a piece of Yes music, it's horrid. At least the ABWH tracks were trying to sound like Yes; this song sounds like it was written with other artists in mind, which it probably was. Be warned if you haven't played it in a while: it is annoyingly catchy.

'Miracle Of Life' (Rabin, Mark Mancina)
Production: Trevor Rabin with Mark Mancina and Eddie Offord
From the ridiculous to the sublime. 'Miracle Of Life', in this author's opinion, must go down as one of the unsung Yes classics (alongside 'To Be Over' and

'Dreamtime' from *Magnification*), even if its organ riff is borrowed from Handel's *Water Music*. It takes the structure pioneered on 'Changes' from *90125* and makes it almost as good. Its exuberant and inspiring introduction features Alan White's best work on the album, while the superb main song sounds as if Jon Anderson were born to sing it. If the band had had time to produce more pieces like this wonderful seven-and-a-half-minute track, the album might have been as good as *90125*. As it is, it's frustrating that this standout piece of music should be surrounded by so much relative mediocrity by an album so full of half-baked songs and disappointing filler.

'Silent Talking' (Anderson, Howe, Wakeman, Bruford, Elias)
Production: Jonathan Elias
At exactly four minutes long, this interesting track again shows what might have been. It has one of only two writing credits for Wakeman on the album and includes some parts that certainly sound like him. It also borrows a riff from 'Sensitive Chaos' that Howe would later use on his excellent solo album *Turbulence*. The track has two distinct parts, both excellent, which feel like they should have been sections of a longer piece, but here the song ends frustratingly quickly.

'The More We Live, Let Go' (Squire, Billy Sherwood)
Production: Eddie Offord and Billy Sherwood
Vocals, bass, guitar, keyboards: Billy Sherwood
As well as working with Rabin, Chris Squire was also developing a working friendship with Billy Sherwood, whose own relationship with the band would develop later. This slow-burn of a song is excellent, with Anderson again well integrated and sharing lead vocals with Squire and Sherwood.

Sherwood also plays almost every instrument, including the bass part, which Squire liked enough from the demo to keep it on the finished song. Given the relative homogeneity of the ABWH songs, this piece really stands out as something special.

That a (then) non-member of the band was given such a prominent role on the album is both gratifying and alarming. It shows how cobbled together a lot of this album was.

'Angkor Wat' (Anderson, Wakeman, Elias)
Production: Jonathan Elias
Cambodian Poetry: Pauline Cheng
Left off the vinyl version of the album with some justification, this largely ambient piece is somewhat forgettable, with some very dated keyboard sounds, and marks a real downturn in the album's fortunes. The subject matter deserved a better piece of music. The piece is named after the Buddhist Temple in Cambodia, thus the additional spoken word recital by Pauline Cheng.

'Dangerous (Looking For The Light Of What You're Searching For)' (Anderson, Elias)
Production: Jonathan Elias
Featured guitar: Jimmy Haun
Guest vocals: Chris Squire
This is a slice of rather dumb pop/heavy rock, with funk overtones. The track was intended to capture the spirit of *90125*, but, in fact, it gets caught up in its own late-1980s/early-1990s production style. It is only notable for some terrific bass work from Tony Levin, his playing at last lifted from the stylistic shackles of being asked to sound like Chris Squire. Jimmy Haun is the featured guitarist and his conventional (but excellent) playing is clearly very different from Howe's.

'Holding On' (Anderson, Elias, Howe)
Production: Jonathan Elias
This is the final 'full band' piece, a rather mediocre affair dominated by Anderson, with some decent work from Howe, Bruford and Levin and a short synthesizer solo from Wakeman (probably), but otherwise, the song is forgettable. It is another that might have been dropped to make the album more listenable as a whole. As the spiritual 'climax' of the whole record, it just isn't good enough.

'Evensong' (Bruford, Levin)
Production: Jonathan Elias
A short and charming instrumental for bass and electronic percussion that is completely wasted at the end of the album. It feels like a prologue to an epic that doesn't exist.

'Take The Water To The Mountain' (Anderson)
Production: Jonathan Elias
This is, let us not forget, the close of many versions of the CD – and of the vinyl version of the album. Again, it's a largely ambient piece with chanted vocals and very prominent electronic percussion. It's actually rather effective, but again as an album closer, it just doesn't work.

Related Tracks
'Give And Take' (Anderson, Howe, Elias)
Production: Jonathan Elias
How ironic that one of the strongest ABWH tracks on the album should be completely missing from the vinyl and international versions. It's an exuberant, up-tempo piece, mercifully free of the production quirks that blight many of the ABWH songs. It makes some nice use of guitar harmonics, and while Haun may well play some of the guitar, it's exciting and powerful without resorting to heavy rock histrionics. Anderson delivers his 'rock' voice

very effectively. If you are outside the UK and have never heard this song, seek it out. It's a little gem.

'Love Conquers All' (Squire, Sherwood)
There are two versions of this Squire/Sherwood song in existence – one recorded during the *Union* sessions with lead guitar and lead vocals from Rabin and the other with Sherwood singing from the Squire/Sherwood *Conspiracy* album released at the end of the decade. The song itself is fine, if hardly earth-shattering, and the Rabin version is marginally the better of the two.

'The More We Live' (Squire, Sherwood)
A later version of the song from *Union*, again from the Squire/Sherwood album *Conspiracy*. Anderson's voice is missed, but the production is smartened up considerably, making this, on balance, a more definitive version of the song, so worth seeking out.

Union Live
Voiceprint
Recorded at Shoreline Amphitheatre, Mountain View, California, on 8 August 1991
Released: 6 January 2011 (one-DVD, two-CD)
Tracklisting:
1. 'Intro/Firebird Suite', 2. 'Yours Is No Disgrace', 3. 'Rhythm Of Love', 4. 'Heart Of The Sunrise', 5. 'Clap/Mood For A Day', 6. 'Make It Easy/Owner Of A Lonely Heart', 7. 'I've Seen All Good People', 8. 'Solly's Beard', 9. 'Saving My Heart', 10. 'Whitefish/Amazing Grace', 11. 'Rick Wakeman Solo', 12. 'Awaken', 13. 'Roundabout'

The eight-man tour of 1991 was enjoyed by audiences and, in the main, by the band. It threw up some interesting personnel dynamics, with Kaye seemingly happy to play second fiddle to Wakeman, while Howe and Rabin seem to have co-existed without any major difficulties. The set fused material from the mixed-era Rabin and classic eras, alongside a few tracks from *Union*. Long sets included solo spots for Squire, Rabin, Howe and Wakeman, plus White and Bruford squaring off in an entertaining duet. Other highlights included Wakeman soloing at the end of 'Owner Of A Lonely Heart' plus a showcase eight-man 'Awaken' to close the main set. Much, although not all, of the tour took place in the round, as had the *Tormato* and parts of the *Drama* tour.

Many shows were available as bootlegs, but no official releases appeared until 2011 with a DVD and double CD release of most of a show in California. This is fine in itself, although it failed to present the whole set; there was a limited bonus DVD recorded in Florida a few months earlier, and there was also video from a Denver show in May.

Voiceprint also released a series of glorified bootlegs from the *Union* tour in 2021, including part of the Wembley Arena show that the author attended in June 1991.

This blurs the division between official releases and bootlegs somewhat dangerously. Nonetheless, the official DVD does give a good impression of the dynamics that made the tour unique.

Above: Trevor Rabin on the *Union* tour, 1991.

What Happened Next?

Although the tour, which ended at the start of 1992, was a considerable triumph, the band were left in a state of uncertainty. Bruford was never a long-term bet, and Howe and Rabin could never have stayed in the same band beyond that live tour. A version of the band with Rabin and Wakeman was initially mooted, but instead an offer came in from Phil Carson for the band to be part of his fledgling Victory label with the *90125* lineup.

This resulted in the excellent *Talk* album, which saw Rabin and Anderson working better in tandem, but fell between two stools – not poppy enough for 1980s fans and not adventurous enough for those for whom *Close To The Edge* was the pinnacle. Worse was to come when Victory folded, and the band limped through a US tour. Rabin took the blame, and the band fell apart again.

Fortunes revived in 1995 when an offer came in via the band's new management to reform with the *Going For The One* lineup for some showcase live shows near Anderson's home in San Louis Obispo, California. These, in turn, led to two batches of new material, released in a somewhat uncomfortable live/studio package as *Keys To Ascension Parts 1 And 2*.

By the time that the second part came out in 1997, and with Wakeman unable to tour the project, the band had again moved on, recruiting Igor Khoroshev on keyboards and bringing in Billy Sherwood, whose material with Squire became the somewhat unloved *Open Your Eyes*.

The band returned to the road, releasing the better-favoured *The Ladder* in 1999. With Sherwood moving on (for now) and Khoroshev being fired after an unsavoury incident on the 2000 *Masterworks* tour, the band recorded *Magnification*, released in 2001 with an orchestra replacing keyboards, and toured it in 2002 with American Tom Brislin on keys. Later that year, Wakeman was back as the band celebrated 35 years with two long tours in 2003 and 2004.

With Wakeman no longer willing to undertake long tours, a planned return in 2007 with his son Oliver was postponed when Anderson suffered a severe bout of illness. This led the rest of the band to move on, recruiting singer Benoit David to replace him. Attempts to record a new album were hijacked by producer Trevor Horn, who brought back his fellow Buggle Geoff Downes on keyboards for *Fly From Here* in 2011. By 2012, David was also suffering health issues and was unceremoniously replaced by Jon Davison, for the lacklustre *Heaven & Earth* in 2014.

That band was rocked by Squire's death in 2015, which was replaced (with Squire's blessing) by a returning Billy Sherwood, while drummer Jay Shellen deputised for Alan White after the latter also suffered health issues and became a permanent member when White passed away in 2022.

White did, however, play when the band were inducted into the Rock and Roll Hall of Fame in 2017, which saw Anderson onstage with Howe for the first time since 2004, having toured as Anderson, Rabin, Wakeman that same year.

Yes now continues with Howe at the helm, plus Davison, Shellen, Sherwood and Downes, and have released three albums since 2021: *The Quest*, *Mirror To The Sky* and *Aurora*. Meanwhile, Anderson is in the midst of a late-career renaissance with his band The Band Geeks, playing a set of Yes classics.

...and that brings us up to date at the time of writing.

Above: A relaxed band promotional shot, circa late 1972 or 1973.

Other Live Albums And Compilations

The Word Is Live (three-CD boxed set, streaming, released 2005)
A very useful resource for diehard fans, this three-CD set includes a mixture of archive recordings from radio broadcasts and private recordings between 1970 and 1988.

The quality is variable, but it does throw up a few choice ditties, such as a cover of 'It's Love' by the Young Rascals from July 1971 (Kaye's last performance with the band), and material from the *Tormato, Drama* and *Big Generator* tours.

Yesterdays (LP, CD, streaming, released 1974)
This was a stopgap release, a best-of culled from the band's first two albums. As well as six tracks that had appeared on *Yes* and *Time And A Word*, it also included 'Dear Father' – then a rare B-side – and the full, 1972 arrangement of 'America', featuring Bruford, Howe and Wakeman. It's also got a slightly risqué cover from Roger Dean. At the time, it was pretty much an essential purchase, and I do indeed have copies on vinyl and CD, but with both the tracks that were originally unavailable only here now widely available elsewhere, it's now something of a 'completists only' purchase.

Classic Yes (LP, CD, streaming, released 1981)
Classic Yes is a single-album by-numbers 'best' of with an attractive Roger Dean cover. Some editions came with a 7" single with two live tracks from the *Tormato* tour: 'Roundabout' in Oakland and 'I've Seen All Good People' at Wembley. Neither track is available elsewhere but is on the streaming versions of the album. The other tracks are all – of course – fabulous, but this is very much a compilation for the curious, not the fan.

Yesyears And Yes – Greatest Video Hits (VHS, later DVD, released 1991)
Around the time of the 1991 *Union* tour, Eagle Vision released two videos. The first was *Yesyears*, a two-hour documentary with some live moments, presenting a diplomatic history of the band using testimony from the eight-man *Union* lineup. It's pretty uncritical, is missing some crucial players – like Banks and Moraz – and hardly mentions the *Drama* era or ABWH at all.

The Greatest Video Hits is more fun – official videos and a few live cuts with jokey commentary filmed at one (or more) of the *Union* arena shows. Kaye and Wakeman are the main ringleaders, though Bruford and Rabin are also good value.

Yesyears (four-CD set, released in 1991)
At the same time as the videos above, Atco released a sumptuous four-CD boxed set, showcasing a new logo (which didn't really 'take') and a terrific full-colour programme-style brochure with a band history. It is mainly a best-of,

with a few interesting additional or alternative versions, particularly from the Rabin era. It includes two live tracks, which come from 1988 on the *Big Generator* tour, and do allow us to hear what sort of fist Tony Kaye makes of 'And You And I' and 'Heart Of The Sunrise' (answer – pretty decent). Overall, it is an invaluable, beautifully packaged set for fans and well worth picking up.

Above: Chris Squire holds court as the rest of the band , including Patrick Moraz, look on circa 1975.

Bibliography

The following books are either essential or useful reading about Yes:

Banks, P., James B., *Beyond And Before – The Formative Years Of Yes* (Golden Treasures Publishing, 2001)
Barrow, S., *Solid Mental Grace – Listening To The Music Of Yes* (Cultured Lama, 2018)
Bruford, W., *The Autobiography* (Jawbone, 2009)
Chambers, S., *Yes – An Endless Dream Of '70s, '80s And '90s Rock Music* (General Store, 2002)
Farley, A., *The Extraordinary World Of Yes* (iUniverse Inc, 2004)
Howe, S., *All My Yesterdays* (Omnibus, 2020)
Kirkman, J., *Time And A Word – The Yes Interviews* (Easy On The Eye Books, 2018)
Lambe, S., with Watkinson, D., *Yes In The 1980s* (Sonicbond Publishing, 2021)
Martin, B., *Music Of Yes – Structure And Vision In Progressive Rock* (Open Court, 1996)
Morse, T., *Yes Stories – Yes In Their Own Words* (St. Martin's Griffin, 1996)
Mulryne, K., *Yes. The Tormato Story* (Self-Published, 2023)
O'Reilly, S., *Yes And Philosophy* (Self-Published, 2012)
Popoff, M., *Time And A Word – The Yes Story* (Soundcheck Books, 2016)
Romano, W., *Close To The Edge* (Backbeat, 2017)
Wakeman, R., *Say Yes* (Hodder And Stoughton, 1995)
Watkinson, D., *Yes – Perpetual Change* (Plexus, 2001)
Welch, C., *Close To The Edge – The Story Of Yes* (Omnibus Press, 1998)

The following more general books also give some insight into Yes:

Bassols, G., *The Musical Instruments Of Progressive Rock* (Circulo Rojo, 2019)
Blake, M., *Us And Them: The Authorised Story Of Hipgnosis* (Nine Eight Books, 2023)
Ewing, J., *Wonderous Stories – A Journey Through The Landscape Of Progressive Rock* (Flood Gallery, 2018)
Horn, T., *Adventures In Modern Recording* (Nine Eight Books, 2022)
Lambe, S., *Citizens Of Hope And Glory – The Story Of Progressive Rock* (Amberley, 2011)
Macan, E., *Rocking The Classics* (OUP, 1997)
Romano, W., *Mountains Come Out Of The Sky* (Backbeat, 2010)
Snider, C., *The Strawberry Bricks Guide To Progressive Rock* (Lulu, 2008)
Stump, P., *The Music's All That Matters* (Quartet, 1997)

Some quotes were taken from *Yes: Classic Rock Artists* DVD (Black Hill)
Rock Candy magazine interview with Trevor Rabin, Issue 83, December 2020

Online Resources

yesworld.com – the official Yes website
yesfans.com – long-running fan site and forum
yesmusicpodcast.com – excellent weekly podcast about the band
bondegezou.co.uk – website of long-term Yes chronicler Henry Potts
forgotten-yesterdays.com – invaluable online resource
setlist.fm – invaluable archive of setlists

Facebook has many Yes-related groups. Join them at your leisure (or indeed peril).

Would you like to write for Sonicbond Publishing?

We are mainly a music publisher, but we also occasionally publish in other genres including film and television. At Sonicbond Publishing we are always on the look-out for authors, particularly for our two main series, On Track and Decades.

Mixing fact with in depth analysis, the On Track series examines the entire recorded work of a particular musical artist or group. All genres are considered from easy listening and jazz to 60s soul to 90s pop, via rock and metal.

The Decades series singles out a particular decade in an artist or group's history and focuses on that decade in more detail than may be allowed in the On Track series.

While professional writing experience would, of course, be an advantage, the most important qualification is to have real enthusiasm and knowledge of your subject. First-time authors are welcomed, but the ability to write well in English is essential.

Sonicbond Publishing has distribution throughout Europe and North America, and all our books are also published in E-book form. Authors will be paid a royalty based on sales of their book. Further details about our books are available from www.sonicbondpublishing.com. To contact us, complete the contact form there or email info@sonicbondpublishing.co.uk